When you ride ALONE you ride with bin Laden

What the Government *SHOULD* Be Telling Us to Help Fight the War on Terrorism

BY BILL MAHER

NEW MILLENNIUM PRESS
Beverly Hills

ISBN 1-893224-90-2

Library of Congress Cataloging-in-Publication Data Available

Art Director: Stephen Edelman
Assistant Art Director: Lauren Alpert Magnin
Book Design: Kerry DeAngelis, KL Design
Jacket Design: Stephen Edelman and Kerry DeAngelis
Jacket Illustration: Rob Fiore
Author photo: Charles William Bush

New Millennium Press
301 North Canon Drive
Suite 214
Beverly Hills, CA 90210

10 9 8 7 6 5 4 3 2 1

First Hardcover Printing November 2002
First Paperback Edition September 2003
Printed in United States of America

Dedication

I dedicate this book to my partner in crime, Sheila Griffiths, and to my friends Michael Viner, Kim Dao and Billy Martin, who also contributed mightily to achieving my completely unreasonable demand to get the book idea I thought of in June out in November.

Also, I am forever in the debt of the talented artists who brought to life the images you see in these posters. As my agent never stopped telling me, "a picture is worth a thousand dollars."

List of Illustrations

Acknowledgements

There are a few people I'd like to acknowledge for making this book possible, and they are:

George Washington; Abraham Lincoln; James Madison; Alexander Hamilton; John Adams; Benjamin Franklin; Thomas Jefferson; General Ulysses S. Grant and General Dwight D. Eisenhower.

And everyone who worked so hard on this project of establishing a free nation and keeping it free. Without their hard work, dedication, brilliance of mind—and most of all, courage—a book like this simply wouldn't be possible.

A Word About Lag Time

Between the time this book went to press and the time it came out, God knows what could have happened. In such a volatile, quickly-changing world, two months is an eternity.

Shortly after 9/11, President Bush said he wanted Osama bin Laden "dead or alive." Then, after we didn't find him, that sort of morphed into, "Well, hey, he's *either* dead or alive!"

I would gladly have the title of this book sound dated if it meant Osama bin Laden was indeed dead. But even if he is, that hardly means the War on Terrorism is over. As James Bond told Goldfinger: "Go ahead and kill me—008 is waiting to take my place."

Table of Contents

Introduction

Making Connections

When the shock of September 11, 2001 wore off and Washington, D.C. went back to what it does best—pointing fingers and renaming things—the phrase we heard over and over with regard to our intelligence agencies was "connecting the dots." The FBI and CIA failed to "connect the dots," the strands of information that warned a real war was about to start with a sneak attack.

But plenty of dots aren't being connected by the average citizen, either, and that's what this book is about: how we all can connect what we do on the home front to quicker victory here with fewer of our servicemen overseas.

Traveling the country, I find that people want to do more here at home, but are at a loss as to what. Even when the government issues a Terrorism Advisory, it's maddeningly vague—"Terrorist alert today! Code Burnt Orange!"

"And what?" I always want to say, "Bring a sweater?"

Of course, there are reasons why the American government no longer helps us make war-related connections, mostly having to do with where those connections might lead us politically. There's a World War II-era government poster that reads "Should brave men die so you can drive?"—a question we might well ask ourselves today. But don't count on the government to ask it, not in an age when campaign contributions from oil companies are so important to getting elected.

And so we're on our own—but that's OK. Because if the government won't tell you what time it is, I will. In the pages that follow are the posters I believe the United States government *should* be making and plastering everywhere, like they did in World War I, World War II and the Cold War. We see in posters from those eras a government unafraid to call upon its citizens to curb travel, save tin, buy bonds, plant a victory garden—whatever it took to make those connections for people, so the average Joe knew what he or she could do to help the war effort.

Of course, this is a very different kind of war, and what we can do to win it is sometimes very different from how other generations pitched in. But the common thread from then to now is the idea that civilian support can be the deciding factor in a war, provided people know what to do. Loving my country as I do, it is my sincerest hope that this book will help.

VICTORY
BEGINS AT HOME
GIRARD
What we do here...
Can bring him home sooner

Make Them Fight All of Us

If you've already given blood and sent a charitable donation directly to Julia Roberts so she can personally hand it over to a World Trade Center victim, and you've already made the tough personal sacrifices outlined by our president—shop, travel, and go out to eat—you may now be asking yourself, "What more can I do to help the war effort?"

What we can all do is show a willingness to change. And I'm not talking about simple, superficial change like putting a flag on our cars or refraining from criticizing the administration. The concept I'm talking about is sacrifice. Some people do it for their families, some people do it to get rock-hard abs, but not many of us seem willing to do it for America.

Americans today confuse freedom with not being asked to sacrifice. The fact that you can't have everything you want exactly when you want it has somehow become un-American. We'd rather sacrifice virgins than our SUVs: "I'll guzzle as much gas as I want—this isn't Europe!" Sure you can, Captain America, but just try to imagine a World War II-era American saying, "I'll use as much damn gas and tin as I want—and while we're at it, screw your victory garden!" They'd call you "Axis Asshole." Somehow, America morphed from a nation that embraced rationing to one that practically impeached Jimmy Carter for having the nerve to suggest we turn down the thermostat and put on a sweater. Even in the wake of an event so invasive and frightening as September 11, not one person in a leadership position in America asked anyone to really give up or rethink anything. Pandering to a spoiled citizenry had become so ingrained, it remained in place even as buildings and complacencies crumbled. "Keep shopping!" the president told us, letting the political chips fall where they may.

"Shop till *they* drop!"

Yes, we were asked to do very little, and we responded. That's the bargain we tacitly make with our presidents: we won't ask too much of you, if you don't ask too much of us.

Especially in these past two decades of unprecedented prosperity, we Americans have come to love win-win situations: risk-free investments, no-pain dentistry, the high-fat diet. We've grown accustomed to success without effort. In operations like the Gulf War, Somalia and Yugoslavia, we got the lowdown on our "war" from the nightly news while continuing to work, golf, build our stock portfolios and enjoy *Frasier*. It's not that we don't care—it's just that we'd prefer not to get involved. We're more supporters than doers, great at the symbolic stuff like flags, ribbons, and benefit concerts. (Sitting through Liza Minnelli *is too* a sacrifice!)

Nothing is really *our* problem—especially when you're talking about an outlay of time or money, or, God forbid, something that causes stress! By Thanksgiving 2001, we were right back to "how to cope" and "things to make yourself feel better." After a hard day of stimulating the economy we congratulated ourselves for getting through this trauma without letting the bastards change the way we live!

You hear a lot of that: if we stop bowling or screwing or whatever it is we wanted to keep doing anyway, then *they win*! And we pretend we're dumb enough to believe that this extends not just to our American virtues, but also to our flaws. We convince ourselves that even our shameless waste, our unchecked consumption and our appalling ignorance of anyplace in the world except our own little corner must continue—*or they win*! No, when you become smarter and less gluttonous, *you* win. We *all* win!

And all of us can, if we want to, have a big hand in winning this war. In World War II, the axis—the original one, not the cover band working today—had to fight *every* American, and they knew it. Civilians, and the level of support they give their protectors, make the difference in war time—a lesson we learned, or should have, in Vietnam. We'd bomb a bridge, and in hours the North Vietnamese townspeople had built a crude but usable replacement. It was sheer hell for our guys because they had to fight the whole country.

Likewise, American citizens today could make things a lot more hellish for Al Qaeda and all the other *als* out there if only we'd get it on a practical level that we're in the war too, just not on the front lines. Israelis understand that and we eventually will too, but not until our government and our media start helping us make those connections between what we do and how it can help our troops—and ourselves—stay out of harm's way.

"We were asked to do very little, and we responded. That's the bargain we tacitly make with our presidents: we won't ask too much of you, if you don't ask too much of us."

When you ride ALONE
you ride with bin Laden!
Join a
Car-Sharing Club

When Sacrifice Was Cool

Perhaps the most threatening of all the connections we're not making these days is the one between terrorism and one of the great loves of the American life, the automobile. Each of us in our own individual high-performance, low-gas-mileage vehicles, exercising our God-given right to drive wherever we want, whenever we want at 0% financing and practically no fuel cost, inadvertently supports terrorism.

When we don't bother to conserve fuel and when we treat gasoline as if it were some limitless entitlement, we fund our enemies, like a wealthy junkie fattening the wallet of his dealer. Maybe not directly—it's not like you'll find Ayman al-Zawahiri making your change in the Plexiglas booth at the Exxon station. But he may as well be, because you can bet Al Qaeda funds their most ruthless operations with money they get from people who sell their oil to Exxon before Exxon sells it to you.

The countries that have the money to offer large cash awards to the families of suicide bombers, or to send little boys to madrasses, the prep schools of hate, are getting that money from people using lots of oil.

Of course, conserving oil by carpooling may sound like a neat idea, and maybe on some level we get it that we'd have more leverage with these terrorist-funding nations if we weren't beholden to them. But actually doing it means we'd have to drive out of our way to pick somebody up and that'll take time and he'll probably wanna talk and I'm not much of a morning person and what if he spills some of his damn mochaccino on my taupe, brushed-leather seats?

Circa 1941-1945, Weimer Pursell. Created by Office of Government Reports. United States Information Service. Division of Public Inquiry. Bureau of Special Services, OWI.

And there's the rub. We are hopelessly, romantically, singin'-in-the-rain in love with our cars. Rather than carpool or improve mass transit to ease traffic and commuting time, we'd rather live in the car and make it more like home: state-of-the-art sound systems, cruise control, telephones, bigger built-in receptacles to hold more food. No wonder Al Gore was ridiculed for suggesting we find a way to phase out the internal combustion engine within 25 years. You'd think he asked everyone to turn in their car keys right then and there, taking away our freedom to come and go as we please and trapping us cruelly in our homes with our spouses. But Gore was right when he said it was a matter of national security.

We used to make that connection, because the government endorsed it. An original 1943 wartime poster warned Americans, "When you ride alone, you ride with Hitler!" Oil was regarded as an essential weapon during World War II, and it is certainly no less so today.

I chose "ride alone" as the title of this book because it not only pays homage to a time when sacrifice was cool, but also warns us in a larger sense what happens when we ride alone. We've become a nation of individuals, accustomed to "getting mine" and "looking out for Number One." Even the Army's recruitment ad shows a soldier running alone and tells you you'll be "an army of one."

But we're locked now in a bitter fight for the very way of life that allows us such indulgence, and victory clearly hinges on whether we ignorantly continue to "ride alone" or rise up once again to stand together.

So remember: when you ride alone, you ride with bin Laden. And that's not an easy smell to get out of your car.

"It's not like you'll find Ayman al-Zawahiri making your change in the Plexiglas booth at the Exxon station. But he may as well be, because you can bet Al Qaeda funds their most ruthless operations with money they get from people who sell their oil to Exxon before Exxon sells it to you."

WE SAY THEY'RE OUR HEROES...

BUT WE PAY THEM LIKE CHUMPS

The Kitchen is Closed

After September 11th, I never much liked the trend of everyone and his brother wearing the hats and jackets of the NYPD and FDNY. Only the people who do the job should get to wear the hat. Would you wear someone else's Medal of Honor?

Yes, it's a tribute, and sincere tribute is always appropriate for these brave people. But wearing their symbols is also rubbing off a piece of heroism that isn't ours. As long as we keep talking about what they did, we don't have to talk about what we're not doing.

And one thing we're definitely not doing is paying the people who do the very difficult jobs we don't want to do. According to the Department of Labor statistics, the national annual income for firefighters in 2000 was $34,000; for police officers, $37,000. The Department of Defense statistics on basic pay for an active duty officer in his first two years was about $25,000. Soldiers living on or near the base in America often need to use food stamps to get by. Teachers in their first year make an average salary of $28,000, and often buy classroom supplies out of their own pocket because there just wasn't any money in "the budget."

"No money in the budget"—we hear that, shrug, and go on, as if it's a cosmically unalterable fact. Corporations do it with their budgets, too. I've seen it in show business. One day, no more coffee and doughnuts for the crew. "The Budget" didn't allow it anymore, like "The Budget" was handed down by God himself and brought directly from heaven on a golden chariot by those bastards who pulled their ads from my show, Federal Express.

Claiming "the budget can't allow it" reminds me of when you walk into a restaurant at a civilized hour like ten o'clock and they say "The kitchen is closed." For years I would hear this, and think, "damn, just a little too late, oh well, thank you, I guess it's Denny's again."

And then one day it hit me: kitchens don't *close*. Just as at home, at a certain point in the night, I stop *using* the kitchen—but at three in the morning, if I want to, I still have the ability to go downstairs and "re-open" the kitchen. By turning on the stove and opening the refrigerator! Restaurants are not banks; at the stroke of ten an enormous airlock doesn't seal off the kitchen and render the preparation of food an utter *impossibility*.

No, kitchens can open and budgets are what certain people say they are. The budget comes from somewhere. There's a line extending from it, like a trail of breadcrumbs, and it leads back to people voting, or not voting, or voting stupidly. Budgets are made by politicians. Or corporations, but that's kind of the same thing. One makes teachers pay for pencils, one takes away coffee and doughnuts.

Because it wasn't in "The *Budget,*" some things have to get cut.

Yeah, some always do. But for years until the accounting scandals of 2002, it never seemed to be the year-end bonuses of already wealthy CEOs, often in the hundreds of millions of dollars. That would buy a lot of coffee and doughnuts.

This is a country that is the richest in the history of the world—a country where middle-class people now commonly use maids and limousines, luxuries that when I was a child were the appurtenances of only the wealthy, never people I knew. It is also a country that is always reluctant to raise the minimum wage because, my God, the cost of the arugula salad at Le Crap might go up from eleven to thirteen dollars, as if anyone who'd pay eleven dollars for a salad would notice.

So what's the connection we need to make here? Again, it's one we really know, the one between how much taxes we shell out and how much pay goes to the people we say are our heroes.

Does government waste money? Of course, mostly because we let them, and frequently even encourage them. (Back home, one man's pork is another man's jobs program.) We all think the government should get by on far less of our money.

But until that miracle happens, the ones who get screwed by tax whining are the cop, the fireman, the teacher and the soldier. We should think about that the next time we put on their hats.

"This is a country that is always reluctant to raise the minimum wage because, my God, the cost of the arugula salad at Le Crap might go up from eleven to thirteen dollars, as if anyone who'd pay eleven dollars for a salad would notice."

Political Correctness is Dangerous...

Demand *Real* Security

The Problem at the Airports

I hate stupidity, but what I hate even more is when people actually brag about it. For example, when America's television stars finally felt it was "emotionally safe" to hold the 2001 Emmy Awards—after a compromise of no tuxes and a somber tone—local news reports ignorantly raved about the preposterously inefficient level of security. They boasted that "even the most recognizable stars were required to present a valid photo ID." Which is exactly what's wrong with America's approach to security: we're so intent on presenting the appearance of evenhandedness, on not singling anyone out or hurting anyone's feelings, that we defeat the purpose. They're celebrating the fact that *it appears* as if they've left no stone unturned and I'm thinking—you have limited resources—leave a stone unturned! *Sharon Stone*, for instance. You can direct your manpower elsewhere because she's not a likely terrorist suspect—she's *Sharon Stone*!

Likewise, Transportation Secretary Norman Mineta has insisted that we must heed the lessons of 40s Japanese internment in not resorting to racial or ethnic profiling in our airports. When asked on *60 Minutes* whether a 70-year-old woman from Vero Beach would receive the same level of scrutiny as a Muslim young man from Jersey City, he replied, "I would hope so," proving that the first casualty of war is common sense. "Passengers should find all the evidence of equal inspection reassuring," Mineta said.

Reassuring? It's reassuring to know that the people guarding our jugular have decided on a policy of suspending human judgment? Actually, having robots and nitwits check everyone equally is a sure recipe for disaster. It's a mindless, exploitable system of window dressing and posturing; it's pro-

Circa 1941-1945, James Montgomery Flagg. Created by Office of Government Reports. United States Information Service. Division of Public Inquiry. Bureau of Special Services, OWI.

cedure-bound automatons following prescribed guidelines by rote. It's random-ness when we need focus. It's heads up asses when we need heads up.

And this is coming straight from the top. President Bush's response to a hissy fit thrown by an armed Arab-American Secret Service agent who'd been taken out of line and questioned before boarding a plane was that he'd be "plenty hot" if he found out the guy was scrutinized because he was Muslim. Which was Dick Cheney's cue to whisper in the president's ear, "Ah sir, that's what Ashcroft is doing *every day*." Sure, it's OK for Ashcroft to inter-rogate everyone who's ever glanced toward Mecca—*his* profiling was A-okay. In fact, if you whined about it and brought up civil rights you were just "aiding the terrorists." But at the airports, where we face the most obvious and imminent danger, we have become dangerously and inexplicably com-mitted to placing pretense over results.

// **President Bush's response to a hissy fit thrown by an armed Arab-American Secret Service agent who'd been taken out of line and questioned before boarding a plane was that he'd be 'plenty hot' if he found out the guy was scrutinized because he was Muslim. Which was Dick Cheney's cue to whisper in the president's ear, 'Ah sir, that's what Ashcroft is doing *every day*.' //**

Somewhere along the line we became this oversensitive victim culture where it is assumed that no one is ever supposed to get physically or emotionally hurt. We can't approach or question anyone about any-thing for fear of hurting their feelings, mak-ing them self-conscious, and ultimately becoming the defendant in their discrimina-tion lawsuit. Remember, we're not talking about beating young Middle Eastern men with rubber hoses or placing Arab-American families into internment camps. We're asking them to perhaps endure a few extra questions at the baggage check-in line so that we can all get back to the days when the most life-threatening thing on a plane was the Chicken Kiev.

The people who hate us target all Americans—black, white, young and old—but just because they're indiscriminate about going after us doesn't mean we must be indiscriminate in going after them. We've been brainwashed into believing that it's a sin to discriminate. But discrimination doesn't mean racism; it means telling unlike things apart. Iowa grandpas and nine-year-old girls from Ohio are simply not looking to visit "a painful chastisement upon the Western infidels." "Profiling," like "discrimination," has become a bad word, even though all police work is based on it, as it must be. If we stopped calling it profiling and started calling it "proactive intelligence screening" or "high-alert detecting," people would be saying, "Well, it's about time."

By the way, passenger searches are not only random, they include random acts of kindness. Screeners are being trained to smile and glance down at the tag on the bag and call passengers by name: "Have a good flight, Mr. Samsonite!" At the Baltimore airport they've hired mimes and jugglers and other *Cirque de So Lame*-type entertainment to divert flyers waiting in long security lines. It's all part of our national policy of placing feeling good over actual safety.

It would be good if we could get with the program. It would be better if we had one first.

Ground Zero

The word people most often use about matters involving a nuclear exchange between warring nations is "unthinkable." Nuclear war is simply...unthinkable.

Yes, it is—which is why we need to think about it. Because it may be unthinkable, but it unfortunately is not impossible. It's barely into "unlikely."

Defense Secretary Donald Rumsfeld told the American people last year, "I think it's unlikely that they have a nuclear weapon, but, on the other hand, with the determination they have, they may very well." And then, to make his point even more clearly, he actually physically covered his ass.

The nuclear threat is real. Enemy sleeper cells almost undoubtedly reside amongst us right now—perhaps targeting reactors or building a device in a Bayonne, New Jersey basement—and our best hope at foiling them seems to be to get Allen Iverson to kick in their door.

One of Osama bin Laden's proclamations in 1998 was:

"We issue the following fatwa to all Muslims: the ruling to kill the Americans and their allies, civilian and military, is an individual duty for every Muslim who can do it in any country."

Gosh, is there anything this guy doesn't love about us?

On September 11, a whole city cared for 3,000. Like many people, I have had a love-hate relationship with New York City for many years, but on that day, you only saw the greatness. Strangers helping strangers, businesses offering their inventory to rescue workers and, in one touching scene, a cab driver stopping to pick up a black guy.

But, just for a moment, contemplate this unthinkable concept: what if the numbers were reversed? What if just thousands were left to come to the aid of an entire city?

I find it disconcerting to hear of the attack site in New York referred to as "Ground Zero," even though the first definition in some dictionaries certainly fits: "the target of a projectile, such as a missile or bomb." However, prior to 9/11, I don't recall ever hearing other non-nuclear missile or bomb blast sites referred to as "Ground Zero." Prior to 9/11, the common usage of "Ground Zero" was the way it's defined first in *Webster's*, "the point directly above, below, or at which a nuclear explosion occurs." We kept that term separate, to remind us that there is nothing like nuclear warfare—nothing.

But a pain-averse culture wants to ascribe a term equal to their perceived distress, and Ground Zero sounds appropriately ominous coming out of Tom and Peter and Dan. Très gravitas.

But ominous and gravitas are actually in the building now. So how about actually doing something about security instead of just appearing to? A new bureaucracy and a color-coded warning system seem like steps in the right direction, and I'm sure both programs tested very well with the focus groups. But we're not unveiling feel-good sitcoms for the new fall season; we're talking about our survival here. When the next fall season rolls around, I'd kind of like to *Be There*.

"On that day, you only saw the greatness. Strangers helping strangers, businesses offering their inventory to rescue workers and, in one touching scene, a cab driver stopping to pick up a black guy."

"THEY HATE US BECAUSE WE DON'T EVEN KNOW WHY THEY HATE US"

A Small Pond

In the months following 9/11, it was the question asked most by bewildered Americans: "Where the hell is Dick Cheney?"

A close second, however, was, "Why do they hate us?" John Powers of the *LA Weekly* had what I thought was the best answer: "They hate us because we don't even know why they hate us."

The United States, as I will attempt to show in the last chapter, has acted with more restraint and non-violence than any other country in history with comparable pre-eminence—but we do ignore people. We are oblivious to suffering. We are cheap with charity if it's not close to our home.

All of which is not nearly as bad as rape and pillage and sowing salt in the earth—and attempts to lay all Muslim problems on "American foreign policy" is pathetic alibiing for not doing the hard work of fixing Muslim society. But what is it that drives haters crazy with rage? Many times, it's being ignored. To a person with pride, being ignored is often worse than out-and-out hate; it's that much more of an insult, that you're not even worth noticing. Or worse, that you deserve to be left in your own ghetto. You see it here in America: once the Persians or Arabs start coming to the disco in numbers, everybody stops going. That has to hurt.

(Not that it's all our fault: Middle Eastern men are just too aggressive with women. They came to the melting pot, but they brought that bad attitude toward women, and girls just don't put up with that shit here. When you come to the melting pot, it's polite to melt a little.)

I was watching *Jeopardy* (home with Mom) recently, and three whiz geeks who knew everything about everything ran the board and made my mother and me feel like idiots. But the Final Jeopardy category was "Countries in Africa," and all three bet nothing, confident that they were absolute ciphers on this topic. They were right; their answers *were* way off. I thought it said a lot about the American myopia that gets under the skin of have-nots, who comprise at least half the world. (Not that they really watch *Jeopardy*.)

And that's just the insult. Then there's the injury itself. "They" hate us because they feel—and "they" are not wrong—that it is within our power to do so much more, and that we practice a kind of passive-aggressive violence on the Third World. We do this by, for example, demonizing tobacco as poison here while promoting American cigarettes in Asia; inflating produce prices by paying farmers not to grow food as millions go hungry worldwide; skimping on quality and then imposing tariffs on foreign products made better or cheaper than our own; padding corporate profits through Third World sweatshops; letting drug companies stand by as millions die of AIDS in Africa to keep prices up on lifesaving drugs; and on and on.

We do, upon reaching a very high comfort level, mostly choose to go from ten to eleven instead of helping another guy far away go from zero to one.

We even do it in our own country. Barbara Ehrenreich's brilliant book *Nickel and Dimed* describes the impossibility of living with dignity or comfort as one of the millions of minimum wage workers in fast food, aisle-stocking and table-waiting jobs. Their labor for next to nothing ensures that well-off people can be a little more pampered.

So if we do it to our own, what chance do foreigners have?

Well, maybe a little more because more of *them* are completely nuts and will do things like, oh I don't know, fly planes into buildings. So we have some self-interest going here, and that's a good thing. Maybe it will make us remember—or learn—that the planet is a small pond, and everything we do has a ripple effect. We tend to follow the lead of someone like—well, our president, who before he attained that office, was known for having very little interest in foreign affairs, and it was not held against him. Most Americans would agree with any good ol' boy who says, "Hey, I'm a good guy! So what if I don't know nothin' 'bout no foreigners. I'm not doing anything to hurt them…."

Well, yes and no. That's too naïve in this global world. Not doing anything *is* doing something, and choosing to look away is a passive but no less mortal sin.

The poster is from a scene in the movie *Apocalypse Now*. Lance, the championship surfer in Captain Willard's outfit, water-skis behind his PT boat on the Mekong River, happy and oblivious to what his wake is doing to the natives. And that's America: arrogant oblivion. Not trying to hurt anyone, but not really caring when we do.

"We do, upon reaching a very high comfort level, mostly choose to go from ten to eleven instead of helping another guy far away go from zero to one."

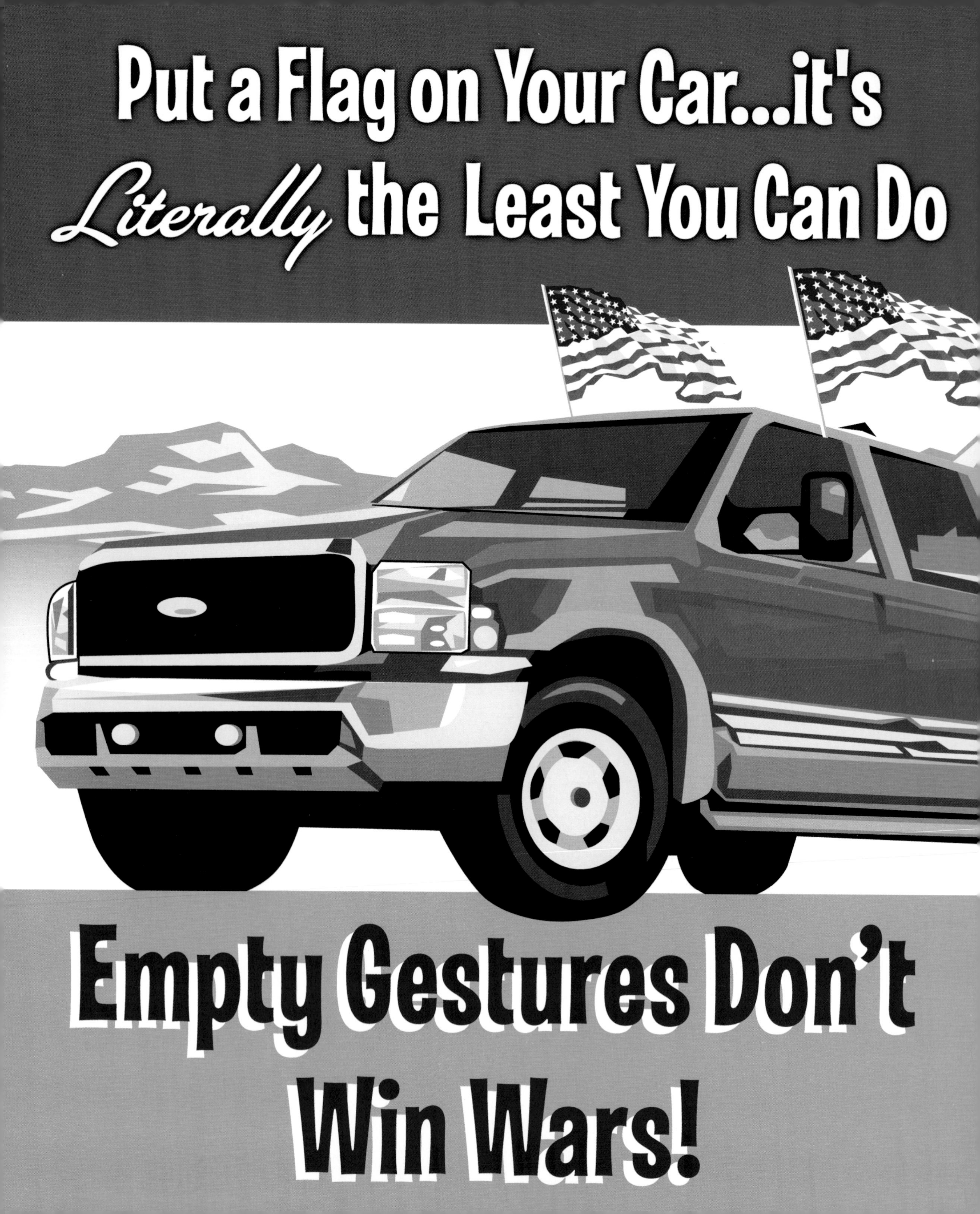
Put a Flag on Your Car...it's
Literally the Least You Can Do
Empty Gestures Don't
Win Wars!

New Glory

After 9/11, there was a lot of talk in this country about a "nation transformed" and "a sleeping giant awakened" and "everyone pitching in." But in the end, what did *we* really do?

We put a flag on our car. (Half of which were manufactured in Germany, Japan or Sweden.) Or two flags, if we were really mad! Big ones, up front, so we could feel like Rommel in his staff car, speeding to meet the Fuehrer.

For months in the fall of 2001, our highways looked like a county fair on wheels. "Look out, Al Qaeda—patriot on board!" I once saw a guy with five flags tell a guy with four flags to go back to Afghanistan.

Now, is there anything wrong with flags? Of course not. I like the flag plenty, but I never forget it's only a symbol, a reminder of what we stand for, not a replacement for actually standing for it. Brave Americans in past wars didn't die for the actual flag—they died for the freedom it represents, including the freedom to burn it. Too many in America lead with their emotions when it comes to the flag, becoming illogically protective. Hell, the British treat *their* national symbol, the Royal Family, way worse, and they're *people*!

> **// Too many in America lead with their emotions when it comes to the flag. Hell, the British treat *their* national symbol, the Royal Family, way worse, and they're *people*! //**

The problem with the flag at this moment in our history is we've become masters at fooling ourselves into thinking there is a way to get everything with very little effort. It's ridiculous we need to even be reminded of this, but just displaying a flag doesn't actually *do* anything, any more than "tying a yellow ribbon" brings home a hostage or AIDS ribbons cure AIDS. If we think we've done something because we went to Kmart and bought a flag, then the flag is actually hurting, not helping us.

True patriotism is doing something for your country. If our car flags had to be earned with real contributions—purchased with deeds, not dollars—if each one we saw meant someone had given blood or volunteered their time or donated money or written their congressman or saved a gallon of gas, perhaps then we'd really be bucked up at the sight of them.

Slaves to Our Freedom

Evolution is about survival of the fittest, adapting to adversity, immunizing one's self from that which poses a threat. And as we begin to recognize our oil dependence as an Achilles heel, well, then I would say it was time for us to do a little evolving.

After World War II, Americans started treating gasoline as if it were a necessary element for sustaining life, like air and water and television. We preach about capitalism and the beauty of unfettered market forces determining price—but not when it comes to gas. When it comes to gas, we need it cheap, and the president had better get it for us, or else, and we don't care how. If it takes a hundred thousand dead Iraqi "soldiers" to keep gas below two bucks a gallon—when the rest of the world pays five and up—*then that's what it takes*! That's the "price" of gasoline. Just look what happens when gasoline prices go up by even a few cents. Americans throw an embarrassingly juvenile tantrum, outraged that they have to think twice before taking the couch-mobile to Wal-Mart for a bucket of Rocky Road and a lawn bag full of potato chips.

It's a funny thing about Americans, we love to bitch about paying too much for things we really need and are really a bargain, like gas and postage stamps, but we willingly shell out outrageous amounts for unnecessary crap like gourmet coffee and soap to make your crotch smell good. Two dollars a gallon to go ten miles is too much, but five to the parking valet to go ten feet is okay.

We should stop worrying so much about the *price* of gasoline and start considering its *cost*. You really want to be patriotic? Don't change your car by putting a flag on it, change the car. Improving our overall fuel efficiency by just 2.7 miles per gallon would completely eliminate our need for oil from the Persian Gulf—you know, where the troublemakers come from.

And until we can wean ourselves off the good, imported stuff altogether—and we'll have to someday—conservation is our only sound recourse. Oh sure, there's our domestic supply, that private bottle we keep in a desk drawer, but even if we drilled in every wildlife refuge and put oilrigs on all our coasts, we'd still only be tapping about 2% of the world's reserves, barely enough to continue producing Astroglide.

And for what? For big, garish wagons that we want to make us powerful, but of course cannot. Stop calling SUVs SUVs, because it stands for "sport utility," and soccer moms and football dads are not using these leviathans for sports *or* utilities. Unlike in the commercials, few people use them to cross the Rockies (because, you know, wherever Lewis and Clark went, ditto the Navigator). In the commercials, every model is "a totally new driving experience." Please—a totally new driving experience would be a car with wings. Does this car fly? Otherwise, everything is still basically a Chevy.

So let's cut the crap: we're driving school bus-sized urban assault vehicles *around town*—and that's just the women. The men want to be rebels. Oh, yeah, you're a sexy, off-road radical because you're in a *Pontiac*. You're not one of the masses! Hey, wouldn't it be great to go to a PTA meeting in a *tank*?! Wouldn't that be the coolest? That's not something everybody could do! Perish the thought of something available to everyone—members only, baby.

And by the way, Selfish Utility drivers: I personally don't want other motorists sitting high enough to see what's going on in my lap.

The irony is what we love most about our cars—the feeling of freedom they provide—has made us slaves. Slaves to cheap oil, which has corrupted our politics, threatened our environment, funded our enemies and had us doing the dirty work for a lot of royalist dirt bags in the Middle East for a long time. It's time we took a good, hard look at our driving, and this is something we have to do for ourselves, because our leaders aren't going to help. They're like the lush on the next barstool who drinks more than you do. Faced with our addiction to oil, what does our leadership say? Get more of it!

Strange when you consider their answer to *drug* dependence is to cut off the supply.

"Two dollars a gallon to go ten miles is too much, but five to the parking valet to go ten feet is okay."

WHICH STONER ARE YOU WORRIED ABOUT?
CANNABIS CLUB
TELL THEM IN WASHINGTON!
PROTECT US FROM EVIL,
NOT FROM OURSELVES

Dope

I could never be a politician for many reasons; one of them is, I like to change my mind. Maybe it's just my feminine side crying to get out, but I do. And in politics you can't, which is so stupid, because it means voters encourage a candidate *not* to grow and think. If you're running for office and your position on any issue has changed the slightest bit since you were in grade school, then you're waffling, and you're forever after labeled a waffler. Even if it means ignoring new information coming to light, *be consistent*. God forbid you read an article when you got into *junior high* that gave you *information that changed your mind*. Changed your mind? In attack ads, you'd find out that's why you *"can't be trusted*!"

The sad thing is, that shit works. The real axis of evil in America is the genius of our marketing and the gullibility of our people. It's a deadly hook-up when you can sell 'em anything, and the American people have been sold drug paranoia so long it's a tradition. Policies based on pure ignorance and fear, with detriment not just to those who get arrested, but to innocent people who never get back their seized property, to kids whose parents go away for smoking pot, to high-crime neighborhoods that go under-policed because the cops are both corrupted by the drug trade and busy chasing the dealers.

We laugh at *Reefer Madness*, like, "wow, how ridiculous people were about pot back then," but we don't deserve to laugh, because nothing has changed.

And why? Because it's an easy political sale. Accusing your opponent of being "soft on drugs" is money in the bank as far as attack ads go—so why not go for it? You're running for office! You have no spine, you just want to be famous and are too ugly for show business! So even though you don't really believe we should be draconian on pot smoking, you'll say that just to stake out that issue in the attack ads. Except then, when you get elected on your stupid ideas, you have to try to turn them into laws. Otherwise, in the *next* election, the asshole you beat with *your* cynical attack ads will accuse you in *his* cynical attack ads of not following through on your campaign promise of the death penalty for anyone with a Bob Marley record.

Early in the twentieth century, starting with a false marketing campaign, Americans abandoned their previous policy of government non-interference in whatever people wanted to do to take the edge off, put the edge on, or get it up—and we've been the worse for it ever since. There are real victims in this Drug War. Where's the *Dateline* frosty lens report on the "pot-smoking Daddy who never came home?!" There's some swing sets going un-pushed in the Drug War, too, if the 700,000 annual pot arrests mean anything.

My last, best hope of ending the Drug War quickly ended shortly after 9/11, when it became apparent that we were all politicians, and *even in light of new information*—you know, the "we're under attack" thing—we still did not "waffle." We stayed loyal to stupidity and the stupid stuff that had always failed, because we're loyal and have honor and integrity. The Drug War would continue!

The Real Axis of Evil in America is the genius of our marketing and the gullibility of our people.

But for a couple of weeks there, I had hope. After all, a new day had dawned, and everyone was in agreement that we'd just gotten our priorities slapped into shape like two weeks at Juvenile Boot Camp. Attorney General John Ashcroft said, "We cannot do everything we once did because lives now depend on us doing a few things very well."

Right on. Cool. Well said. The guy really gets it.

Except, of course, he doesn't, and didn't really mean it. Cut to February 12, 2002, the target date for the most specific FBI-issued terrorist warning since the 9/11 attacks. This was before the color-coded alert system, so it was somewhere between "Heads up" and "Danger, Will Robinson!" And where were our federal authorities? Well, at least some of them were kicking in the doors of California medical marijuana dispensaries for AIDS and cancer patients. They didn't catch any actual hijackers, but they did nab a guy named Jack who was high.

On that same day, President Bush announced, "If you're buying illegal drugs in America, it is likely that the money is going to end up in the hands of terrorist organizations," echoing the television ad campaign that premiered two weeks earlier on the Super Bowl—because those Super Bowl ads are *real* cheap, so what a good use of terrorist-fighting money!

It was all part of the administration's plan to piggyback their Drug War agenda onto the blank check of support they were receiving for the "other" war—you know, the one everyone was *really* behind. In making political headway, "for the war" had become the new "for the children."

But in the same way our airport security suffers when we spend finite time and manpower pretending everyone is equally likely to blow up the plane, so does our defense suffer when we pretend the drug trade is the real piggy bank for crazy

Arabs. It's one thing for our American government to have abdicated the role of helping citizens make connections in time of war, as we see they have. But it's even worse when the government purposefully misleads the public to the *wrong* connection. You actually do more to support Al Qaeda by driving when you go out to pick up your drugs! Hell, all of us can help by driving less but, unfortunately, not everyone has a smack habit to give up. (And among those who do, is "George Bush really wants you to!" going to be the thing that makes a junkie quit?)

No, the target of drugs as faux terrorist-connection #1 was chosen because it's *politically* perfect—truly, a dream come true for any administration's top spinmeister, because it:

a) targets something—drugs—that has been successfully demonized, certified evil from decades of marketing.

b) asks absolutely nothing of 99.9% of the people because *heroin* is the only drug that really benefits terrorists, so when even a crackhead hears "drugs fund terrorism," he can say "well, he's not talking about *me*!" and:

c) it takes the heat off the oil companies, who make a hell of a lot more campaign contributions than drug dealers.

Which is not to say that contributions from more than a few drug dealers haven't slipped through over the years. They have, but then the candidate has to send the check back and pretend he really cares where the money comes from.

I promise you, he doesn't. Oil companies, car companies—that's a big chunk of the economy, and a lot of contributions. Not to mention that we Americans love our Lincoln Navigators, so that leaves the druggies to take the heat on sacrificing for the war… at least until we can find a way to blame it on the smokers.

Oh, by the way, if you're looking for an actual connection between drugs and terrorism, there is one, but it's a little Six Degrees of Kevin Bacon. You see, the religiously conservative Taliban forbade involvement in the heroin or opium trade. It's the Northern Alliance—you know, *our* allies—who cultivate and deal in the substances that find their way to America under such colorful names as China White and Tango & Cash. But hey, ally, enemy—minor point when you've got the evil of drugs working for you in the ad campaign.

Just as long as we all know: the President should conceivably be calling on Americans to support our allies by *increasing* their heroin use. Where's the ad that says, "Hey America, why not switch from that skunky-tasting import beer…to smack?"

What has to Happen?

Where's the Outrage?

I think we need to change that old saying, "I don't need a building to fall on me," because two did and we still don't get it.

We all do it, of course. Sticking one's head in the sand is a deep human impulse. Like when you feel some kind of bump or growth on the back of your neck, and your heart jumps, because, Christ, that could be something bad, I should see a doctor right away! But then you don't, because it's too scary, and what if they do find something, and...and besides: *maybe it will just go away*!

Hmm...something growing under my skin...bubbling up from inside me somehow...literally a problem coming to the surface: let's make that our very sixth priority!

People are funny about warnings and precautions. Warnings can be frightening and imposing and require action—who needs that hassle? Remember Jeffrey Dahmer, the homosexual pedophile who killed and ate his victims? Months before his eventual arrest, an Asian teenager—a male Asian teenager—came running from Dahmer's apartment naked, bleeding from the rectum and pleading for police officers to help. The cops wrote it off as a likely "domestic disturbance"—you know, naked, in shock, bleeding from the rectum—just another gay tiff. No red flag there. Yet the press found a story where Jeff Dahmer was caught sneaking into the Honor Society photo every year in high school, and they made it seem like *that* should have been the red flag.

How did we not see it coming?! Sneaking into the Honor Society photo, eating Asian

Circa 1914-1918, James Montgomery Flagg. Created by Mayors Committee, 50 East 42nd Street.

teenagers—duh! It was an obvious, desperate cry for help, and now we must ask ourselves, "What can we do to *make sure it never happens again*! Stricter policing of Honor Society photo sessions! I challenge my opponent to sign a pledge making it a federal crime for anyone caught sneaking into high school photo sessions, and if he doesn't sign it, he'll be *threatening our children*!"

(By the way, hack politicians promising to make more and more crimes federal is one reason the FBI didn't have time for terrorism. But hey, carjacking is down 2%.)

// With all due respect to the poor souls who didn't deserve to die in New York, a successful breaching of America's defense core—speaking from reason and not sentiment—should be more worrisome. //

In a similar way, why do people act shocked whenever NASCAR drivers get into an accident or die—what?! No! Wow, one minute he's flying around an oil-slicked track at 200 mph, bobbing and weaving between cars, and the next minute: gone! He was standing right next to me an hour ago, and then he got in the car and...fate, huh?

Yeah, that one came out of the blue, but remember the American nuclear submarine that surfaced directly under a Japanese fishing boat, killing nine? *That* we have to stop from happening again. Like it ever would. Have you been on an ocean? It's big. It's literally an ocean of water. That a Japanese fisherman could awaken one morning as he does every day and by lunch have a Los Angeles Class Attack Submarine up his ass just means a certain allowance for fate must be accorded. America is bad at discriminating between danger likely to strike again, and red herrings, the freakish helpings of disaster that no man or plan can prevent.

Having the Pentagon attacked is a red flag, not a red herring. The flag does not get redder or realer than that. With all due respect to the poor souls who didn't deserve to die in New York, a successful breaching of America's defense core— speaking from reason and not sentiment—should be more worrisome. It should serve as the highest possible warning of danger. The World Trade Center was the one that got more attention, and aroused more feelings, so of course the media loved it. But attacking the Pentagon? That's our defense department—the castle keep, the place that's supposed to be secure within the secure place. It's threatening your queen in a very direct way. When the enemy gets to your citadel, your prided epicenter, everything's in play.

When the Vietcong ran amok in the capital of South Vietnam in the 1968 Tet offensive, that was when people here started to really freak out about the war, and rightly so. But Tet, and Walter Cronkite's pronouncement after it that the war couldn't be won, probably changed American minds of that era more than this brazen attack on our own capital today. Two months after Tet, a sitting president who loved the office and the power abdicated. People were mad at him, and he knew it. I'd like to see a little more of that anger from people now. Anytime we find out that the fight against terrorism is being shortchanged by politics and greed we should bare our teeth at Washington.

We should have done it a few times already, and we haven't. For example, when in December, 2001, President Bush said "civilization is at stake," that was just one week after announcing that if Congress asked for more than the $40 billion earmarked to fight terrorism, he'd veto it. So, while pledging $140 billion to a no-strings-attached tax give-back to corporate campaign donors and $5 billion to an airline bailout, we capped "civilization" off at a non-negotiable $40 billion.

The brave Argentinian author Jacobo Timerman once said, probably from his jail cell, "It is very easy to hate a Nazi, a guardian in a Gulag. But the real danger is not them. It is the decent people who compromise with evil."

Eric Hoffer said, "The mystery of our time is the inability of decent people to get angry."

I realize that sadness is a much safer emotion, but is it necessary to have so demonized anger in America?

"McCain? Hey, doesn't he have a temper? Yeah, I think I read that—ooh, I don't know about him. Can you trust a guy who gets mad?"

Can you trust a guy who *doesn't* get mad? Let's *get* a guy with a temper. Maybe spending five years in a box in Vietnam makes a man a little cranky. But it also gives you firsthand experience with "evildoers," and maybe we need a little more of that.

WHAT WE NEED:
A SECRET SERVICE
FOR THE PEOPLE

FIORE

The Solution at the Airports

As of the day this book went to press, there has not been another terrorist attack on the United States since 9/11—but that, I'm afraid, has more to do with them reloading than in us fixing our security gaps. At the airports, you'll find a true Potemkin Village for the nuclear age—all bells-and-whistles and papier-mâché masks, helmed by power-obsessed rent-a-cops who treat passengers like crap and act like they're being heroic in doing so. Only in America do we have troops with unloaded rifles at an airport, then turn our ire to the press for giving that secret away to the terrorists. We waste so much anger in America. Of all the things we waste prodigiously in this country—food, energy, money—that one bothers me the most. We're a complacent society, hard to get riled up in the first place, and then when we do, it's misdirected.

Since we're fond of pretending in America that the president isn't above any one of us, let me pose this question to stir a little ire: why does he get professional security, and we don't? OK, maybe in the past, but now that 9/11 has shown that civilians are in play—why don't *we the people* have a Secret Service, too? A discriminating professional force to guard the places where large crowds gather—airports, seaports, train stations, stadiums, etc. Smart, serious people who know, like the president's detail does, what they're looking for. Why do we get stuck with minimum-wage Richard Jewells asking lame questions that can be answered with a lie?

"Did you pack your own bags?"

"No, Allah packed my bags. Can I go now?"

And looking at driver's license IDs? Oh, yeah, they can never be faked. The *president's daughter had one*! And by the way, terrorists' IDs very rarely say "Carlos the Jackal" right on them.

Our security should consist of trained human behavioral experts who know how to read body language, eye contact, and voice inflection and how to conduct a rapid-fire, on-the-spot grilling. If such a force had been in place on 9/11, the plot would have been foiled. A professional with a trained eye, seeing an angry, twitchy prick like Mohammed Atta, eyes darting and hyperventilating on the airport courtesy tram, would have targeted him immediately for questioning. You don't have to be Mannix to figure out maybe we should have looked into why this guy had a one-way ticket.

But we didn't on September 11, and I don't see evidence it's gotten much better since. Our front line of airport defense can't tell a Mexican from an Arab any better than they can tell a dirty bomb from a disc player—anyone darker on the color chart than George Hamilton gets pulled out of line more. That's as close as they come to "detective work." (Not incidentally, a corps of knowledgeable interlocuters would be better also for the vast majority of non-threatening Muslim-Americans, who would greatly benefit from contact with security personnel who could also tell who the bad guys *aren't*.)

// Our front line of airport defense can't tell a Mexican from an Arab any better than they can tell a dirty bomb from a disc player—anyone darker on the color chart than George Hamilton gets pulled out of line more. That's as close as they come to 'detective work.' //

A Secret Service for the people would be much like the actual Secret Service: a well-dressed, well-paid, elite unit—part soldier, part policeman, part detective, and part psychiatrist—who, like the president's posse, realize there's no time to stop and search everyone individually and no sense in directing their attentions randomly. They'd know how to scan a crowd, identify incongruities, and sniff out trouble, all while watching but not being watched.

And we don't even have to make this up as we go along—Israel already does it, we could just copy. Ben Gurion, Israel's international airport, is the safest airport in the world, and El Al the safest airline. The only complaints they get are about the size of the portions. A full 50% of the people working at Ben Gurion are involved with security in a skilled, highly-respected Secret Service force much like I've been describing. These aren't part-time, desultory, GED-hopefuls juggling offers between life and death security work and Arby's—they're educated, astute professionals, many of whom are ex-army intelligence officers. They work efficiently, but almost invisibly, on high alert, treating each and every day as if there *is* going to be an attack. Like rappers.

Remember our famed shoe bomber, Richard Reid? He flew El Al the year previously and his look, background and demeanor caused concern and special treatment—as well they should have! Did you see the picture of this guy? Sorry, but creepy is creepy, and for ages and ages civilized human societies understood you hire "detectives" who *detect* creepy and check it out to see if it's harmless creepy or something to worry about.

In 1986, a young, pregnant Irishwoman named Anne Marie Murphy was about to take an El Al flight from London to Tel Aviv. Israeli profilers interviewing her learned that she had a Palestinian boyfriend and, again, being *detectives*, were wise in the ways of the world. They knew a woman in love is capable of doing anything for her man, and there are men in this world who can get a woman to do anything. They're called pimps.

And Anne Marie Murphy's pimp, the Israelis discovered, had unbeknownst to her planted plastic explosives in her suitcase. Another terror act aborted where it should be, in the first trimester.

These are the comforting success stories I'd love to hear coming out of LaGuardia, O'Hare and LAX, instead of the one about the woman suing over the humiliation of having a nitwit baggage screener pull out her vibrator.

And that's the part of this that really breaks my heart—that this country, which has so many bright people in it, and could act so smart, so often acts so dumb. It's not like we don't have the brainpower here to pull it off, we most certainly do. But truth be told, we are often, as one president feared we would become, a "pitiful, helpless giant."

The government should be appealing to our best and brightest, asking them to rise to this challenge, but also paying them well to do so. You get what you pay for, and we need to make the connection between the sorry state of our security and our greed; our baffling reluctance to pay for the really important stuff for fear of dipping into profit margins.

If we paid 10,000 highly professional agents $100,000 a year, it would cost one billion dollars. One billion—Congress tosses around bigger figures than that for combating the boll weevil. The Pentagon loses that much before lunch every day.

We all need bodyguards now. Can you honestly think of anything we could better spend the money on?

The Silent Majority

F Scott Fitzgerald has an indispensable quote: "The test of a first-rate intelligence is the ability to hold two opposed ideas in the mind at once and still retain the ability to function." Or as I like to call it, "O.J. killed his wife, *and* the police are corrupt."

I bring this up because fear and war make people single-minded, and it's the worst time for it. For example, criticizing America doesn't mean we want them to win—we want *us* to win, that's why we're criticizing! I care about making *my* country better.

When I criticize Bush, there is never a doubt in my mind, I like him better than Mullah Omar.

One mind, two things—here's another one: while it's true that most Muslims or Arabs are not terrorists, almost all the terrorists are Muslims or Arabs. The question, therefore, is: upon which one of these independent facts do we concentrate more heavily right now? Is this the time for Muslim and Arab-Americans to be grousing about profiling and tolerance? Or is it a time to stand up and be counted as among those patriots uniquely qualified right now to render service to their country?

On the morning after the 9/11 attacks, San Antonio-based Saudi national Dr. Al Badr al-Hazimi was arrested at his home and hauled off by federal authorities, mostly due to the fact that he had the same last name as two of the hijackers. Completely innocent, Dr. al-Hazimi had his home searched, was told his visa was revoked and was transported, under guard, to the East Coast for a week of constant interrogation before he was cleared. And when it was suggested to Dr. al-Hazimi that he was owed an apology, he said, "With all respect, I might disagree…because it is not time to point fingers and to apologize. It's time to cooperate with officials…" In other words, in a time of heightened alert and national crisis, Dr. al-Hazimi chose to practice tolerance rather than demand it.

Contrast that with the story of the Arab-American Secret Service agent I mentioned earlier, the one who got a lawyer and held a news conference. He made a big stink and demanded an apology because an airline temporarily refused to board him, proving, once again, every flight has a crying baby. He was an Arab with a gun, and he took exception to being pulled aside while his credentials were checked. He's willing to take a bullet for his country, but a flight delay is apparently out of the question.

Later, the agent's lawyer said their goal was to make sure this sort of thing "does not happen again." Right. That's the lesson we want the airlines to take away: if an angry, armed Arab flashes a badge, wave him on and get in the sky, because we don't want a lawsuit.

> ## " Let me put it bluntly: the Japanese-Americans in World War II got it far worse, and still gave far more. "

Let me put it bluntly: the Japanese-Americans in World War II got it far worse, and still gave far more. Throwing people in camps and asking them to step out of a line at the airport are not quite the same thing. And yet, the Americans of the 40s who were of Japanese descent refused to give in to self-pity. They just wanted to prove they belonged here, yes, even though it wasn't fair. Life isn't fair sometimes, and no amount of government, litigation or whining can make it fair.

After his ordeal, Dr. al-Hazimi said, "Given the circumstances and the unusual situation, my treatment was fair." Now, there's a phrase you rarely hear from Americans: "given the circumstances"—to say nothing of "my treatment is fair." We have become so hyper-entitled to our individual liberties and our personal rights, so conditioned to automatically put ourselves before the greater whole, that we forget tolerance works both ways, that all of us have the freedom and perhaps the duty to choose to endure heightened scrutiny "given the circumstances." How about some tolerance for our extremely reasonable suspicion that the terrorist is more likely to be both Arab and Muslim, being the people in the world who hate us and are *doing something about it*!

Those clinging to political correctness even in an age of war like to bring up the example of Timothy McVeigh—you know, the all-American terrorist, who shows us it could just as easily be the guy with the blonde crewcut. Yes, it could be, but not just as easily. You can get wet by a single raindrop in a sunshower or by a tidal wave heading toward you. Only fools treat them equally. Timothy McVeigh was a lone wolf, supported by *maybe* 5,000 fringe militia types, whose ranks have since thinned due to over-masturbation to gun magazines. 5,000 people in the whole world who thought McVeigh's philosophy and methods were sound, and only a handful who would actually help out.

But how many Muslims around the world—in Egypt, Pakistan, Indonesia, Gaza, and Saudi Arabia—think what bin Laden has been doing is a good thing, and would love to help out? He's the big seller on T-shirts, that ought to tell you something. People don't wear Timothy McVeigh T-shirts in America, but Osama bin Laden is, for a people who don't have too many recent heroes, Michael Jordan, Bill Gates and Batman all rolled into one. And as long as his face is hanging from the mirror in guys' cabs in Jordan, it means bin Ladenism is mainstream.

It's time we insisted that the Muslim silent majority, the one that claims to abhor Islamist fanaticism and its message of hatred and violence, stop being silent on this issue and actually say so. Say it out loud. In newspapers, and on Al Jazeera, and in the public square. Yes, some people will get jailed and even killed for speaking out, but change comes no other way. Bloodless revolutions are rare. Somebody has to stand up and produce a play as offensive to Allah as *Piss Christ* was to anyone in America who lives above Canal Street. Somebody has to do Chris Rock's act for Arabs.

The first duty within any group is to police itself. Right now, the Muslim world is like a neighbor family who have a rotten teenager named Fundamentalist Terrorism living in their house. He's terrorized the neighborhood, torn up our lawns, and threatened our children. But he's a real thug, and he's still living at home, and the rest of the family is terrified to confront him.

But it's *their* job to confront him—not ours.

And now our message is clear: "Either you control him or we will."

And as long as you don't, all Muslims are somewhat complicit for not speaking out, just the way German civilians who could smell the death camps pretended not to and went on baking bread.

But it doesn't have to be that way. The opportunities for heroism are astounding for Muslim-Americans right now, and an opportunity for heroism is not a gift to be taken lightly. Our CIA, to take just one example, is way behind in this battle, because they put too much faith in technology and too little in the human element. But the human element is right here, living among us. Some hear that phrase—"living among us"—and think "fifth column." But it wouldn't take much to have us thinking "heroes."

And so, Muslim-Americans, I say to you: join the FBI. Join the CIA. Join both, and never talk to yourself again.

But join.

We can't stop doing Cocaine...
So they have to stop living
DEA
FIORE
WHY THEY HATE US

Crazy Talk

It's important to remember as America focuses on the Arab world as our prime terrorist threat that just because other people aren't blowing themselves up to get at us, *that's just lucky*. Just lucky the African or Filipino or Mexican temperament—or religion or history or whatever—hasn't taken them in the "72 Virgins" direction, too, because the hate is present on every continent, and some of it is justified.

Here's one example: we've spent billions on something called Plan Colombia, which, if you're not familiar, allows you to get the first 12 CDs for just a penny. Actually, it's a scheme to address our mammoth coke jones by defoliating the coca fields of Colombia. We love coke, so you get agent-oranged—sound fair? U.S. planes have thus far showered defoliant on more than 200,000 acres, killing not just coca plants but entire ecosystems: damaging legitimate crops, poisoning water supplies, killing fish and livestock, uprooting entire villages, and causing people to suffer fevers, diarrhea, allergies and rashes.

And that's why they hate us: because, to keep drugs out of Bobby Brown's glove box, we kill peasants in Putumayo. If we did this kind of thing to the Arabs, they'd actually have the kind of beef with us that they think they do.

By the way—not that you probably couldn't have guessed this about a government plan—it doesn't work. When a coca field is successfully sprayed, of course the farmers simply move their operation to another valley, like a Whack-a-Mole game. Not to mention that we're sending military hardware and "advisors" into the middle of a convoluted civil war with two leftist guerilla armies fighting the government, right wing paramilitary forces fighting the guerillas, and civilians trapped in the middle. It's Vietnam in Spanish.

But hey, it's got to be done, because some of the plants that grow in the southern hemisphere are just plain evil. We know that because they're not stamped with labels like Bristol-Meyers Squibb, Eli Lilly or Pfizer. And it's vital that we understand that these southern hemisphere plants and their cultivators are to blame, because the alternative is to believe that our national appetite for drugs is our own problem. And that's just crazy talk.

Like any addict, when it comes to the Drug War, the United States is in full denial. What our posturing, moralizing leadership pretends they don't know is that if it wasn't Colombian cocaine, it'd be Bolivian cocaine, and if it wasn't that it'd be homemade methadone or a forty or glue or stolen pills or pot or ecstasy. It'd be *something*, because the mind is a terrible place to be stuck sober. The Department of Stopping Fun can show me all the statistics in the world about how usage of a certain drug has dropped off, but what they never tell you is it's because people found something else. They always will. Whether you call it wine, women and song, or sex, drugs and rock 'n' roll, humans like certain pleasures, and it's really not worth making whole countries hate us by "fighting" something so deep. People like to alter their mood, mostly because other people screw up the planet with dumb laws and dumb decisions that just make you have to do *something* at the end of the day.

"That's why they hate us: because, to keep drugs out of Bobby Brown's glove box, we kill peasants in Putumayo. If we did this kind of thing to the Arabs, they'd actually have the kind of beef with us that they think they do."

THE REAL
CELEBRITY DEATHMATCH
JESUS
MOHAMMED
Religion Can Be Dangerous

"The Man" in the Sky

Having always defined political correctness as the elevation of sensitivity over truth, and being an optimist, I guessed that after 9/11, Americans would judge all matters "PC" to be an indulgence herewith unaffordable. Boy, was I wrong.

Which is bad, because political correctness is much more dangerous now than it was before 9/11. What were once the kind of lies we told to spare anyone's "feelings" from ever getting bruised are now revealed as blind spots in our rationale, inhibiting our ability to fully grasp our predicament.

And there's nothing more politically correct than pretending religion is always a good thing. Saying someone is religious is heard in most of America as a compliment, a reassuring affirmation that someone will be moral, ethical and, after a few glasses of wine, a freak in the bedroom.

People say "I'm a Christian" the way certain politicians say "I have integrity," like we're all supposed to be impressed and back off and kneel down to that almighty testament to naiveté and hypocrisy. When people brag that they have religious faith, I hear "stupidity." Faith is saying, "I will ignore my God-given gifts for discerning reality and instead throw my lot in with blind belief in something that was forced into my head before I could even think."

Isn't that how we get adults in this world who fight wars based on which contrived fairytale they were brought up on? Which desert mirage they were programmed to see—the magic apple and the talking bush or the flying horse and circling the black rock?

But hey, "You have to respect people's religion!"

Why? I don't. I don't respect thinking that is dangerous, prejudicial, childish and could get me killed. And to pretend, as we are apparently supposed to, that the terrorism we face today is not about religion is like saying AIDS in America has no relation to homosexuality. It'll get you applause on *Oprah*, but it's not true. Also an applause line but complete bullshit is "this is not a clash of civilizations." Of course it is, as every major war is. The Civil War was a clash of civilizations, and we didn't even leave the country.

To hear people the week after 9/11 constantly talking up the need for *more* faith and the importuning of *our* God was, to me, the very definition of being "part of the problem." Of course, we in the West like to pat ourselves on the back and say we're more tolerant, and we are—but tolerance is not the same thing as acceptance. It just means, "We think you're crazy and going to hell, but we won't kill you for it—we'll *tolerate* you. But you don't know who the Man in the Sky is, and we do."

// To pretend, as we are apparently supposed to, that the terrorism we face today is not about religion is like saying AIDS in America has no relation to homosexuality. It'll get you applause on *Oprah*, but it's not true. //

Our own president said during the 2000 campaign that he didn't believe one could get into heaven if not a Christian. He had to backpedal on it because non-Christians vote, but millions of Christians who aren't running for anything would endorse that view wholeheartedly.

And why wouldn't they, since they treat the Bible like it's some kind of...bible, and in it there are the words: "I am the way, the truth, and the life: and no man cometh unto the Father but by me." Not a lot of wiggle room there. Put that next to "There is no god but Allah, and Mohammed is his prophet," and it's pretty much "pick a side." One lane open on the highway to heaven.

Of course, when you shut off your brain from rational analysis, *any* book is dangerous. Taking literally ancient parables from thousands of years ago is much more dangerous than playing with a loaded gun. Ancient scrawls, written by different authors in different centuries with different agendas—yeah, let's get mad-literal about *that*.

The literalness problem is compounded in religion by the circular logic of not being allowed to question anything, or else you're lacking faith. Christianity and Islam both have strict bans on of any sort of questioning of the religion itself—or, as the wizard once put it, "Pay no attention to the man behind the curtain!" In the Bible, it's "Don't eat from the Tree of Knowledge," but the meaning is the same: "The stuff we're telling you is going to seem crazy, but *just buy it*."

Imagine being able to sell any other product like that—by insisting the customer swallow every word you spoke about it as gospel or else he'd *burn in hell*. Where you, as the customer, having been brainwashed from birth about the superiority of the product, upon reaching thinking age, forfeit the benefits of the product if you doubt it in any way, and the claims of the product cannot be tested until after you're dead.

Maybe that's why "Religion" is a magic word that allows priesthoods to do anything they want to people. The Taliban kept their women in beekeeper suits. The Catholics got away with *fucking kids*!

If Islam was seen as an ideology instead of a religion, it'd be easy to point a finger in the face of the enemy. But with a religion, no matter how vicious, it gets a little touchy, because, again, we'd hate to come off as intolerant. So we'd like to make it clear that this is a war on terror, and there's no need for us to go digging into exactly where all the hate is coming from.

But, if you must know, it's coming from the Koran or, more accurately, a conveniently literal interpretation of the Koran that informs the impoverished and the frustrated and the humiliated of their righteous duty to strike out, to kill, to wage jihad in the name of their God. The Koran's "Wherever you are, death will find you out, even if you are in towers built up strong and high," does not mean "fly planes into buildings" any more than the story of the tortoise and the hare means "rabbits are losers"—but it's *religion*, so we have to *respect that*, and take it *literally*.

My personal savior is common sense. And as far as God goes, I prefer to believe in one that would want me to use the excellent brain he gave us all.

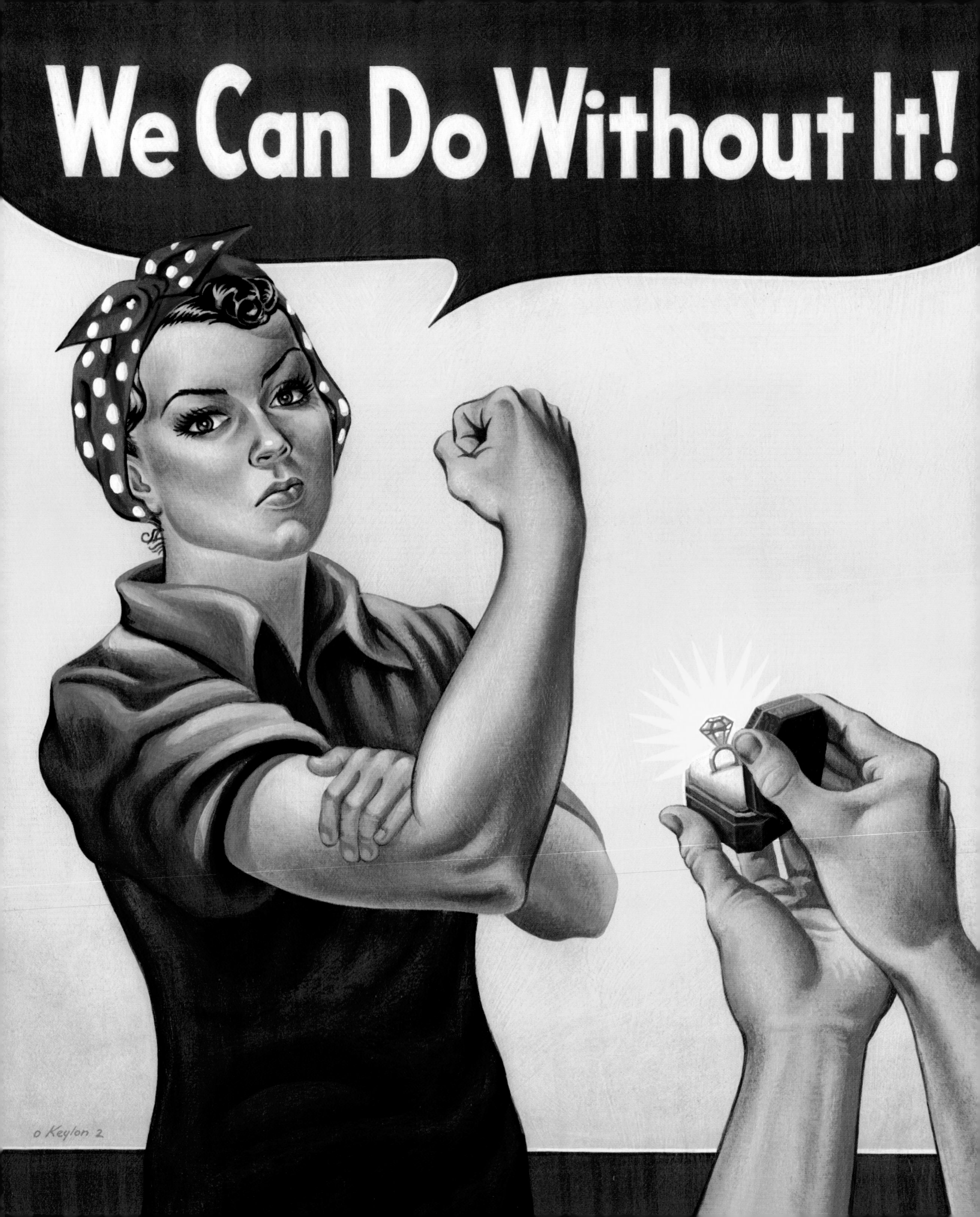
We Can Do Without It!
o Keylon 2

The Oxygen of Terrorism

Until warfare becomes completely automated, women will never do as much as men in war. Men are physically stronger, and so we need them out front and on the battlefield more. That's just reality, and any arguments to the contrary are politics.

But when called upon in America, women have given 100% of what they can give, which is enormous and essential. Just like in the workplace, women who are good workers are the best workers.

But give up diamonds? That's a gut check for women today, who might want to compare themselves to women of another generation, that of my mother, who was an Army nurse in World War II and never expected diamonds, let alone worried about giving them up.

Colin Powell said, "Money is the oxygen of terrorism," which is Secretary of State talk for "It's all about the Benjamins." And terrorists don't use banks or securities, which are assets that can be frozen. They're crazy, not stupid. And they don't hide it under their mattresses—we've seen the caves. No, the bin Ladens of the world take their dirty oil money and convert it into dirty, untraceable things like diamonds. Diamonds are small, easily smuggled, not stopped by metal detectors and can't be identified by dogs—although they can be sniffed out by women from 1,000 yards: that's over nine football fields to you and me.

Not only are diamonds a perfect way for terrorists to launder their money—it's the one thing they do launder—but diamonds

Circa 1942-1943, Howard J. Miller. Created by War Production Board.

actually appreciate in value, so the bad guys see a profit when they convert their diamonds back into cash. So, guys, when you're buying her that diamond to tell her "you'd do it all over again," you might be enabling the terrorists to do it all over again. A diamond may be forever, but terrorism, promiscuously funded, will be too.

Let's make the connection clearly by tracing the path of the diamond. Diamonds start out in the earth, and eventually that earth is part of a country, like Sierra Leone, Angola or the Democratic Republic of Congo. In those countries, desperate battles for control have been going on for decades, and the armies that fight the battles finance their ambitions with diamonds. Villagers are forced to mine the diamonds by ruthless rebels who maintain order through terror: by raping the women and hacking off the limbs of the children—something, by the way, you never see in the DeBeers ads. The rebels then smuggle the diamonds into neighboring dictatorships in exchange for guns and cash. There the diamonds are sold to the highest bidder—whether they be terrorists or "legitimate" dealers—and finally they're laundered in Europe, shipped to America, and end up in jewelry stores where they're purchased by men and given to women in exchange for oral sex.

In the feminized nation we live in, it's practically national policy that women are more evolved than men—but if that's so, how come they're still so impressed by shiny objects? Women complain that men are mesmerized by big breasts, but unlike diamonds, which are a commodity, at least breasts are natural. Well, not so much in L.A., but in general.

I know, it's hard. Women think about diamonds like men think about sex. Like leeches think about blood.

I once told a woman—who happens to be one of the nicest people ever, who only lives to help injured puppies and lonely children and old people—about the horrible situation in Africa with the diamonds. I told her about the rebels, and how they cut off the arms of children, all so they can control and sell diamonds.

My friend looked sad and forlorn. And then, in a tiny voice, she asked me:

"Both arms?"

"Diamonds are sold to the highest bidder—whether they be terrorists or "legitimate" dealers—and finally they're laundered in Europe, shipped to America, and end up in jewelry stores where they're purchased by men and given to women in exchange for oral sex."

REAL PATRIOTS
PAY U.S. TAXES

AWOL

In the months following 9/11, many were labeled traitors by our government: "American Taliban" John Walker Lindh, "American Al Qaeda" Jose Padilla, and "Senator" Tom Daschle. It was easy to point an accusing finger at the very apparent traitors, those who had taken up arms against this country or, worse yet, dared to question the administration.

But just off most of our radars and just off our shores lurk our not-so-apparent traitors, the U.S. companies who have set up shop in the Bahamas and elsewhere to avoid taxation. It's called "tax motivated expatriation"—a nice corporate phrase for "freeloading"—and it's a tax code loophole that allows U.S. companies to enjoy all the benefits provided by their government without the nuisance of having to pay for them. Like stealing, but without the masks.

Of course, these "American" companies don't actually have to move to the Bahamas, which just shows you how dumb they are: the money gets to live in the Caribbean, they stay in Newark. They just have to set up a P.O. box on the island—essentially a phone and a monkey, with some kind of mailbox to collect their dirty, bloody money.

And I do mean bloody. I'd bet that money, or the desire to keep it, has killed more American soldiers than the Iraqi army ever will. Folks of a certain age will remember a play, *All My Sons*, and I remember the movie on TV, with Edgar G. Robinson as the wartime airplane manufacturer who scrimps on the making of certain bolts that then cause planes to crash and pilots to die, among them his son. But, of course, too late he realizes they were *all* his sons.

That might have been a good movie to see for some of the folks running Eagle-Pilcher, the maker of the batteries for our smart bombs, since employees have come forward to accuse the company of allegedly rigging computers to show live responses from dead batteries, faking test reports, and gluing up cracks in battery casings to save the company hundreds of thousands of dollars. Which would have been great business savvy—"How does *Vice President* Martin sound?"—if the faulty batteries hadn't made the smart bombs dumb and caused the friendly fire deaths of several U.S. troops in Afghanistan.

But the corporate mindset in America isn't really that different from the mayor in *Jaws*. Yes, there's a shark out there, but don't tell people! Then the worst possible thing will happen, and we'll *lose business*!

It's practically our national credo: "What's good for business is good for America!" Well, no. Fraud can be good for business; sweatshops are good for business; children work *cheeeap*! The tax cheats in the Caribbean who are AWOL (*Assholes With Official Leave*) love to give you that malarkey about how, without the taxes, they can cut the cost of the product they're making. Yes, and slavery's a real cost-cutter, too. The Civil War was the original "it's the economy, stupid."

Besides, the money isn't really getting trickled down anyway. The ratio of CEO compensation to average worker salary in 1980 was 42. In 2000, that gap had grown more than tenfold, and a CEO made 531 times what the average worker does.

Rich people did very, very well in the last two decades—Reagan and Clinton were a golden one-two economic punch for the wealthy. But now it's time to give back and not forget that that kind of wealth was only made possible because it was accrued in a country that, with all its flaws, is the envy of the world precisely because we have functioning government agencies, like the IRS, that allow people to conduct commerce. Without the S.E.C. and the Federal Reserve, not to mention the FBI and a kick-ass army, the conditions for amassing wealth simply wouldn't exist. But some people always want to argue the bill. Even in wartime.

The IRS estimates that this offshore tax dodge siphons $70 billion each year from our U.S. Treasury, which is approximately our entire tab spent on the Terrorism War the first year.

The connection we have to make here is this: Politicians respond to pressure. If they don't think the people are outraged about something, it slips off their agenda. There are fundraisers to attend, lobbyists to entertain, and mistresses to screw. We have to let them know in Washington what makes us mad at home, and this kind of nonsense certainly should. Any idiot can win votes coming out against taxes—we all hate taxes, we all hate the IRS. But many nations would love to have an effective way of collecting legitimately needed tax revenue—and, unfortunately, with highway robberies like this, we're becoming one of them.

"Of course, these 'American' companies don't actually have to move to the Bahamas, which just shows you how dumb they are: the money gets to live in the Caribbean, they stay in Newark."

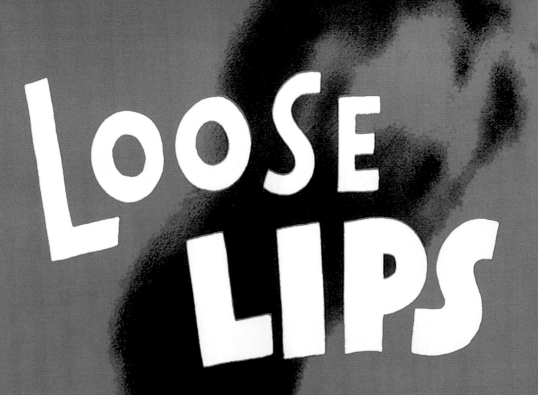

Neighbors Looking out for Neighbors

In many ways, 9/11 was like one giant school shooting, with those who felt persecuted and humiliated lashing out at their perceived bullies. Also, there was a lot of self-recrimination in American society afterward about the warning signs we should have seen. Arab men in flight school advertising that they didn't need to learn how *to land* the plane—that's the "making pipe bombs in the garage" for the terrorist set.

The hijackers lived amongst us without fear of being stopped before they struck, and that's pathetic on our part. Pathetic that after the first World Trade Center bombing and the second Steven Seagal movie about terrorists, vigilance was still neither asked for by the government nor volunteered by the people. The bad guys shared apartments with little or no furniture, and mouthed off about their plans when they got drunk on "virgin scouting trips" to strip bars. Although in all fairness, who knew in a strip club what they meant by "collapsed erections?"

Of course, you could say that hindsight is 20-20, and at the time America was concerned with much more pressing matters, like who'd win *Survivor,* the break-up of Anne and Ellen, and getting Gary Condit to give in and let us smell his finger.

Luckily, it's officially a whole new world now. Just as Columbine ushered in a new era where it's okay for kids to rat on each other, taking seriously and reporting violent threats from fellow students, we all now have a duty to report suspicious activity. We get it now that the world is a dangerous place, and we can't tiptoe around national security.

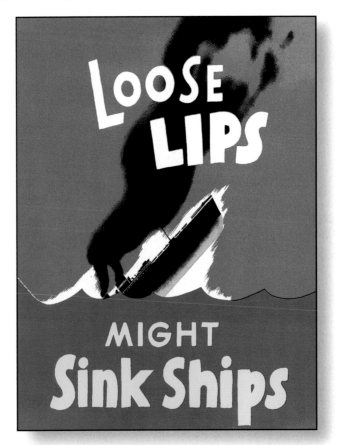

Circa 1941-1945, Essarrgee. Created by Office of Government Reports. United States Information Service. Division of Public Inquiry. Bureau of Special Services, OWI.

If only. A few weeks after 9/11 and just before Halloween 2001, when there were official warnings about possible terrorist attacks on our malls and anthrax was the new AIDS, a retail store clerk in Hackensack, New Jersey noticed a "foreign-looking" man buying $7,000 worth of candy.

$7,000. That's a lot of treats. No one wants their lawn TP-ed, but come on.

So something in the clerk's brain—oh, let's call it reason and the human instinct to survive—superseded his indoctrination in politically correct America to die rather than risk offending someone, and he dropped a dime. The candy bulk-buyer was questioned and cleared by the FBI and sent on his way, his name never released—although a source tells me it was Wen Ho Lee.

Many, of course, went to the old playbook about the evils of profiling, as if pulling over a black guy because he's driving a Mercedes in East St. Louis is anything like having suspicions about someone buying $7,000 of candy right before Halloween when we're on high alert!

It's great to be color blind, and ethnic blind, and religious blind—but blind is blind. It means you can't see. I'd rather see and then judge, as opposed to cutting off the cognitive process quite so early. Why suppress what separates us from the lower forms of life that can't think and replace it with modes of non-reason, like political correctness, term limits or "zero tolerance?"

Look at the World War II posters: we used to be able to trust our citizens to be our eyes and ears. But then again, we used to have common sense, and hold it in some esteem. Political correctness is almost always the opposite of common sense. It's what has us pretending at the airport that Ray Charles is just as likely to blow up the plane as the guy with the bin Laden lunchbox. I'm not saying turn in everyone with an accent and a bad attitude—we'd have no cab drivers. And I'm not suggesting that the government monitor our every move and habit. That's already being done by the credit card industry.

I'm just saying that it takes neighbors looking out for neighbors, and a postman passing along the fact that at 180 Maplewood, the seven addressees all named Mohammed are building "something" in their living room. If it turns out to be just a pole for strippers they get back to the house (the 72 virgins is more likely), then at least we know they're just perverts, and not terrorists.

Like the lady said: it takes a village.

"It's great to be color blind, and ethnic blind, and religious blind—but blind is blind. It means you can't see. I'd rather see and then judge, as opposed to cutting off the cognitive process quite so early."

Dark By Choice

In his baby-on-the-tracks metaphor, ethicist Peter Singer maintains that, if given the choice between saving a third world baby or their new Mercedes, people in wealthy nations would save the Mercedes. Oh, we *say* we'd save the baby, but we remain willfully ignorant of the connections that make such disparate pleasures as diamonds and farm subsidies bad news for dirt-poor Africans, Asians and Latin Americans.

Americans are very touchy about being called cheap and uncharitable. That we are the most generous of givers is a myth you disabuse at your peril, so let me dive right in: Americans will give, but not very far from home, and it better have a good story or personal touch: Parkinson's research if Michael J. Fox gets it, Jerry's Kids after a three-day weekend of badgering, illegal immigrants if they're cute, age seven and their mom died on the trip over.

Giving new meaning to "me," Madonna once said: "AIDS is the greatest tragedy of the twentieth century," which I'm sure came as a surprise to a lot of Holocaust and cancer victims—*but they didn't have to keep replacing so many gay back-up dancers in the 80s*!

We don't feel for anything we have to reach too far to feel for—foreigners, animals, pot smokers—those causes are nowhere, have no power. I've heard many people say with a straight face, "Look how we helped Afghanistan."

Well, yeah, *after* we had a few buildings knocked down over here. Before that, I don't remember a lot of protests and bumper stickers calling for the end of the Taliban thugocracy.

We give 0.01% in non-military foreign aid per year of our budget—dead last among the rich industrial nations, and less than Elton John's monthly Visa bill. The average voter, thinking foreign aid accounts for 15% of our budget, wants to cut it down to 5%, which would be many times what it is in reality. How can a supposedly smart country operate so often in shadows of ignorance this thick and this dark?

My friend Michael Moore once asked, "Will we ever get to the point where we realize that we'll never be safe as long as the rest of the world is living in poverty so that we can have nice running shoes?"

And not just sneakers. When Professor Singer says we'd really save the car, what he's talking about is things like the Farm Security and Rural Investment Act of 2002, which provides $181 billion in free welfare to prop up grain and cotton prices and buy the love of rich, campaign-contributing American agribusiness (which pretends to be the Joads, but really is Archer-Daniels-Midland). This, of course, creates a glut on the market, artificially driving down prices and crippling African farmers' chances of exporting their way out of poverty. The cotton breathes, the Africans not so much. And the food? Let's just say lots of food rots here, on purpose, to keep up prices, while other people starve.

American politics causes a lot of deaths overseas. Whether it's continuing to cripple the Cuban economy in order to buy votes in Florida (does anyone outside of Little Havana give a rat's ass if we trade with Cuba?), or supporting politically generous pharmaceutical companies in their quest to keep prices up and out of reach of all but a few African AIDS patients, politics and money trump foreign life.

So are we really that evil? Actually, no. I don't feel as guilty as some whites about the colonial past—mostly because, not being a racist, I believe humans of all races have the same amount of good (some) and evil (a lot) in them. If the Africans had been more technologically advanced, they would have done it to us—look at Rick James. They certainly did it to their own people, because it wasn't whites who were capturing the slaves in the African interior and bringing them to port.

But that was then, before enlightenment, compassion and kinder-gentler came along. Also, mostly, before awareness. Even a century ago, places like Africa were out of sight, out of mind. They really did call it "the Dark Continent."

But today we live in a global village. It's a continent dark *by choice* now. We can see what's going on all over the globe, and instantly. And the people in those villages, and big cities, know we can see, and they know we could do more if we cared to.

What they are saying about Americans is: "It would cost them so little of their comfort to alleviate a great deal of the abject misery in the world…but even a little bit is too much for them." We're the rich guy flipping a quarter to the starving multitudes, claiming to be "Christian," and saying, "Hey, it's not my fault you're starving."

Which is mostly true, it's not our fault. But that doesn't mean we're still not pricks for giving only a quarter.

The restaurant in the World Trade Center was called Windows on the World. We should take the hint.

"Americans are very touchy about being called cheap and uncharitable. That we are the most generous of givers is a myth you disabuse at your peril, so let me dive right in."

1961

Today

"I believe this nation should commit itself to achieving the goal, before the decade is out, of landing a man on the moon."

— May 25, 1961
President John F. Kennedy

"I believe this nation should commit itself to achieving the goal, before the decade is out, of being completely independent of foreign oil."

—

We Did

We Could

The Empty Podium

Back in the late 50s, the only American we were really able to envision making it to the moon was Ralph Cramden's wife, Alice. But President Kennedy saw the space race as one we couldn't afford to lose, and before we even had a monkey or an ex-Nazi working on it, Kennedy set the lofty goal of a lunar landing and challenged Americans to meet it.

Remember, "Ask not what your country can do for you, but rather what you can do for your country"? Kennedy was unafraid to call upon Americans to sacrifice, pitch in, and demonstrate duty toward country—and Marilyn Monroe bought it.

In today's America, presidents fall in love with high approval ratings, which are usually a good indication they lack the balls to do what's right. True leadership is getting people, despite the political consequences, to follow you down the right path—not waiting to see what path they intend to follow and then running behind shouting encouragement. Kennedy did it with Civil Rights, turning the "Solid South"—solidly Democratic—into a Republican bastion because he insisted that, a hundred years after the Civil War, yeah maybe it was time to make the Southerners start treating the Negroes like human beings.

LBJ did it in Vietnam. He believed in the domino theory, that if we didn't make a stand somewhere, all of Southeast Asia and God knows what after that would fall to Communism. "If you don't stop 'em on the porch, they'll be raping you in your bedroom," he said. And the guy who wanted more than anyone to be loved by everybody gave up all hope of anything close to that by doing what he thought was right.

Was he right about Vietnam and the dominoes? Different issue.

The point is, a leader does what he thinks is right, not what he thinks the popular thing is. One of the great myths of American life is that this is a democracy. It's not. It's a republic, and none of the founding fathers that we revere so much thought it a good idea for the people—the mob—to run the show. Participate, yes, through *representatives*—but then keep clear while they led. Washington, D.C. was founded far from—at the time—the centers of commerce and population. That was on purpose.

A true leader now would tell Americans the unpopular truth: that we use too much energy, that we are spoiled children whose appetite for oil is making us weak and vulnerable. The current administration has not done that. Quite the opposite, they maintain the fiction that drilling for new oil is the only way to ease the choke hold of OPEC. A missile shield—the invisible space diaphragm that's never come close to working—that's top priority for the Can-Do Club. But electric and hybrid cars? Still the stuff of futuristic fantasy in Washington, even though over 50,000 people already drive them.

If President Bush came out today for exploring alternatives to fossil fuels and for cut-backs in our oil consumption, we Americans might finally grasp the gravity of the situation. Bush, after all, is the perfect president to make such a plea, because he *is* Big Oil. He was an oilman himself, from an oil family; all his friends are in oil; he's soaking in it right now! Like Nixon going to China, he could take on the issue with unparalleled credibility, not to mention admiration. I myself, soon after 9/11, voiced the hope that our young president might, like Shakespeare's Prince Hal, transform from the callow youth to the mature vicar of reason and purpose.

"Presume not that I am the thing I was," he might say as he shed the veneer of corporate shill and took up the mantle of wartime leader.

There's still time, but not much.

"Kennedy was unafraid to call upon Americans to sacrifice, pitch in, and demonstrate duty toward country—and Marilyn Monroe bought it."

Why We Fight

When Your Only Right is to Remain Silent

I can't say for sure, but I'm pretty certain that if a woman in a small town in Pakistan or Iran or Syria called the police and said, "My husband is hitting me," the cops would say...

"And? Your point is?"

To get away with that here, you have to be a celebrity or an athlete. But females in even the most advanced Muslim countries are simply, by law, not the equal of men. And I'm not just talking about the extremist interpretation of Islam where women are treated as property, must wear head-to-toe burqas, and cannot work or attend school. In most Muslim countries, the Koran is not just a religious text like our Bible, it's a book of laws and an official government handbook. And the Koran's ideas about women are fifteen hundred years old, like Tony Curtis's. It defines women as the property of men to be "maintained" and physically disciplined. Put it this way: you're not going to see the Koran on Oprah's Book Club.

As I've said, we *are* in a Clash of Civilizations, and nowhere is that more clear than in the treatment of women. I sometimes look at pictures of women covered with tarps like the infield at Fenway Park, and I think: What if these were black men in some white country? Black men being beaten for showing an ankle or a wrist? Black men dying because it was against the law for them to receive medical attention? Black men starving to death because they weren't allowed to work or stoned to death for having sex? There would be protests, riots, U.N. boycotts. Jesse Jackson's head would explode. Al Sharpton would call a press conference.

Isn't it time we stopped ignoring the elephant in the living room and let go of our fair-minded fantasy that all religions are basically the same and that other cultures that suppress human rights aren't inferior, they're just different? Excuse me, but primitive is primitive. The Sudan and Ethiopia and many other countries still practice the genital mutilation of women. The Hmong tribe in Laos observe "marriage by capture," which is a really nice way of saying rape. Remember that Vietnam movie with Sean Penn and Michael J. Fox where American soldiers abduct the pretty teenage girl "for a little R&R?" It's kind of like that, except there's no Michael J. Fox around to decry that people know about it and "they *don't care*!"

But really, do *we* care? Isn't it time we asked ourselves, are we willing to accept any behavior codified within religious or cultural practice? Is there no line to be drawn? If honor killings are okay, then why not virgin sacrifices or cannibalism or sex with children outside the church? We have perversely taken our notion of tolerance to such extremes that we've become tolerant of intolerance.

In the interest of our own preservation and safety, we have to pull back the veil from Islam's face and see it for what it is, not just a religion but a philosophy that fuels the fire of anti-Americanism, an ideology that, like communism, is in theory benevolent and humane but in the hands of many people, vicious, repressive and deadly. When making a stand against communism, we didn't defend it as a peaceful idea that had been hijacked; we didn't pretend that it wasn't dangerous just because we hoped most people living under it would rather be free like we are. We fought it.

> **// No one has to be doomed by faith forever. You can change the fairy tale people need to get through the day. People are sheep, and can be driven to a new pasture. //**

Not that Americans are clean on the issue of women, and a little perspective is in order. Women are also property in our bible; adultery is a property crime in the Old Testament, not a sex crime. Or this: I'm a middle-aged American writing in the year 2002, and when my mother was born, women in America couldn't vote. Slavery was abolished in 1865; women began voting in 1920. We are ourselves relatively new to this tolerance game, and shouldn't act like the recent immigrant who tells the even more recent immigrant to "go back where you came from." We're all lucky in America that we live in a society that does change and grow and self-corrects. Societies can get stuck in a ditch; Islam has been in one for a while, although not for lack of brains or ingenuity or passion. Traditions bind people, and then change comes slowly.

The frustrating thing is, it doesn't have to. Mankind has shown the ability to change, and change quickly. An entire society's long-held, core beliefs can be obliterated in a decade. Following World War II, Japan was occupied and the emperor was forced to announce over the radio that he was not, in fact, God—a title, along with others in his portfolio, emperors had been claiming since the third century.

How's that for a "I never had sex with that woman"? Talk about needing a spin doctor!

"It has come to my attention that mistakes have been made by some overzealous members of the Royal Court, two of the finest public servants I know, and while I knew in my brain it was not the right thing to claim to be *the ruler of the universe*, my heart told me differently, and when I said I 'was' God, it depends on your definition of 'was'..."

But in just ten years, the Japanese were crazy in love with a new girl, capitalism, and in twenty they were beating us at selling our own stuff, like radios and TVs. No one has to be doomed by faith forever. You can change the fairy tale people need to get through the day. People are sheep, and can be driven to a new pasture in a short amount of time.

Kemal Ataturk did it in Turkey—ruthlessly, I'm sure—but in a decade's time, he yanked an entire nation out of the Middle Ages and religious servitude and set them on an opposite course from the rest of the Muslim world. Turkey banned the fez and the veil and made citizens take surnames. The Islamic calendar was replaced with a Western one. They abolished religious laws and polygamy, instituted a secular justice system, and gave women rights. I'm sure that Ataturk broke more than a few eggs making this little omelet, but sorry, I'm a fan. His giant country had—almost literally—no more than a toehold in Europe, and he still managed to pull it to that side of the Bosporus.

And in the long run, don't many more people die and suffer from *not* having that painful modern-ectomy performed on their body politic?

Any society needs what women bring to the party; it's too vast a contribution to do without, being, you know, *half of the population*. And while I don't subscribe to the silly American pandering (which I believe is also the law now) that women are superior, neither are they inferior. The Muslim world will never catch up until they learn to use all their "manpower," including what's under the tarp.

And Americans will never be able to truly count themselves on the side of human rights as long as so much of the world—hardly just the Muslims—continues to get away with systemic, society-sanctioned mistreatment of women, under the guise of cultural differences. Americans should never stop being proud that the soldiers of our army were the liberators of Afghanistan. Once there, we assessed the situation for what it was: Afghanistan was the battered wife, the Taliban the abusive husband, and us the cops. We came, we bombed, we put our necks on the line, and the wife beating stopped. According to my comic books, the guy who comes in and kicks the ass of the "evildoer" is the superhero.

2017

You know how there's a part in every book where the author asks you for money? There's not? Well, there is now.

And it's for a good cause—a charity I'd like to start called "Change for Change," which would collect everyone's pocket change before they went through the airport metal detector, and use it to help fight the War on Terrorism. Right there, on one of its front lines, the airport.

The first question I asked, and kept asking, after 9/11 was: "Can we change?" Can people still change enough to survive, which is what animals do—smart ones, anyway. Which part of our polarized human mind is going to win out—the part that's smart enough to invent nuclear weapons, or the part that uses one to get to heaven?

I worry that the powerful human tendency *not* to change, to stay with the devil you know, is ill-suited for an age of such rapid movement. Maybe centuries ago you could leisurely evolve over time—but with loose nukes and crazy people who want them, I'm for getting our act together fast.

But fast isn't what government does in America. Food we do fast. Dry cleaning, if you believe the sign. But for the United States government and the citizens who move it, it may take more than September 11 to start moving quickly. To give just one horrifying example:

Two months after the attacks, on Veteran's Day 2001, another plane mysteriously fell out of the sky in Queens, N.Y., leading many to wonder if there might have been a bomb planted on board, not a far-fetched scenario since 90% of the luggage in America was still going unscreened. And there was as yet no system in place matching passengers with their luggage. However, spirits had been raised just the week before when, responding to pressure from 9/11, the FAA announced that screening would be fully operational in *2017*.

I'm not kidding, that was their target date. 2017. A mere sixteen years—why, the same amount of time I believe it took Hannibal to cross the Alps. But hey, planes into buildings, planes into houses—what's the rush?

No screening till 2017, but the mimes and street performers were in place relaxing people, and security personnel were now on orders to address passengers by name with a smile. Because, as you know, some time ago in America we decided it was more important to be nice than right.

But then, on September 11 everything changed, except it didn't.

But it needs to, and that's the driving idea behind "Change for Change." So if someday soon you see a bucket with those words on it, give it up. The line will move faster with nothing to retrieve (and also if everyone in America wasn't Mr. and Mrs. Howell and would just *pack what you need*!) Do you really want to hold the rest of us up over your precious seventy-seven cents? If you really need a sticky fistful of coins that badly, maybe you should skip the trip and go back to work.

If nothing else, when people see the "Change for Change" bucket they'll be reminded that security in America has to change, that we can't have everything we had before *plus* the new thing we need now: better security. Sorry, not a win-win—so few things ever really are. We're going to have to *lose* a few things that we've come to enjoy, like total convenience and political correctness.

It's the best thing you can do right now with your change at the airport. Because you do know those nuns are fake, right?

"That was their target date: 2017. A mere sixteen years— why, the same amount of time I believe it took Hannibal to cross the Alps. But hey, planes into buildings, planes into houses—what's the rush?"

IT'S NOT A NEW WORLD

WE JUST JOINED IT

No Security

The 2002 Winter Olympics in Salt Lake City was the site of an odd controversy—and, for once, it didn't involve figure skating. At the opening ceremonies, the Americans insisted upon carrying the tattered Ground Zero flag of 9/11, as if to say to the world, "Lest we never forget…what happened a few weeks ago."

Or, more accurately, "what happened to *us* a few weeks ago." Because—let's face it—that was the subtext: "We're special and when something bad happens to us it's worse than when it happens to you." Name a nation that does not have its share of tattered flags? The Jews and the Irish, to pick the two random peoples I come from, have drawers full of them. Everyone does. The march of history is a bloody mess—I doubt if Monaco has been spared. But no one else imposes their torn laundry and tragic past on this dumb luge and kettle-bowling festival.

I will never believe that what happened on 9/11 was justified, or that those people deserved to die, but I sure do understand how carrying on like American lives hold more value than lives from anywhere else is annoying to the rest of the world. And there's no denying that's exactly what we do. Certainly the media presents it that way, and being the media, I have to believe they're pandering to what people want, which apparently is always saying things like: "A cyclone in Bangladesh killed 80,000…*two were Americans*!"

Right after 9/11, the blow-dried twinks who pass for sages on television were fond of saying "It's a whole new world," when, of course, it's not, we just got a taste of the world as most people have been experiencing it for a long time. I heard a "man in the street" in Cairo—or maybe it was Jalalabad—say "Now Americans will know what it's like to live life with no security."

And that's true, now we do. But we should have known that long before September 11. Certainly the bombing of the embassies in Kenya and Tanzania— that *is* U.S. soil—should have been a wake-up call…buuuut, the bodies being pulled out of the wreckage were black and African, so…hey, who's Pam Anderson dating now? Unless Connie Chung can do a lip-biting "profile" of the victims, it didn't really happen.

Blacks *here in America* can relate to that. Remember when Columbine freaked out white, middle-class America, and the people in the inner cities were saying, "Hello!? Guns-in-schools equals *bad*, thanks for catching on when it's about *you*."

Compounding the affront is the self-righteous posturing our faux-spiritual country constantly puts on display. We talk a good game about God and religion and mankind and humility, but in reality it's a lot about God blessing *America* and really thinking the Jews got it wrong, *we're* the chosen people. It's like the whole country is Marin County.

Leaving the question: Does God make humans or Americans?

In *Broadcast News*, William Hurt, as the bimbo newscaster of his era, asks Albert Brooks, "What do you do when your real life exceeds your dreams?"

"Keep it to yourself," is the reply.

If you're an American born in the second half of the twentieth century, you're lucky. You've won the world power ball lottery. But have some humility about being born on third base. It might help keep the heat off the rest of us.

"We talk a good game about God and religion and mankind and humility, but in reality it's a lot about God blessing *America* and really thinking the Jews got it wrong, *we're* the chosen people. It's like the whole country is Marin County."

A Game of Inches

Bad analogies bother me, none more than those that were spawned by the War on Terrorism. Timothy McVeigh isn't like bin Laden; asking Arabs to answer a few questions at the airport isn't like putting Japanese-Americans in camps; and September 11 isn't like Pearl Harbor.

In 1941, the bombing of Pearl Harbor was the worst possible thing that an enemy could do to us. There was no larger-scale option that might have wreaked even more havoc and taken even more American lives.

Not true of 9/11. Despite the staggering death toll and the incredible damage, planes-into-buildings is paltry compared to what the enemy might have pulled off. In this nuclear-biological warfare age, there is no margin for error.

History is a game of inches. We beat Hitler to the atom bomb by probably not more than months (and probably because he drove a lot of smart Jews over here in the 30s—the only known time in history someone has been punished for mistreating Jews).

We don't know how many inches nearer the haters are today to having the kind of weapons that will get a guy *72 thousand* virgins! It's hard to scare people who want to die, but except for a thin layer of the real fruitcakes, even most nuts and zealots can be scared into behaving, and we need to do some of that. They said Saddam Hussein was crazy when the Gulf War began, but actually, he loves his job, and he wants to keep it, along with his ass and arteries, so when it was made clear to him "you go biological, we go nuclear," he got sane real fast. The Japanese were notorious for welcoming death until Hiroshima and Nagasaki showed them what it looked like on a massive scale. And the reason no one has fired off a nuclear missile in the fifty-seven years since Nagasaki is MAD—mutually assured destruction. Key word: *assured*. That's right, assured, as in, "please, let me *assure* you, if you kill a lot of us, we'll kill all of you—rest *assured*."

Terrorists only understand the cold, unforgiving hammer of brute force. Sorry, but we need "MAD for Muslims." The terrorists threw a good scare into us, but now we have to scare them and the people who help them. If I were the president, I would stretch the already accepted Bush Doctrine of "any country that harbors terrorists will be considered terrorists themselves" to include "any nation harboring a terrorist bringing a nuclear bomb into the United States, even if it's brought over in a PBS tote bag, will be considered to have fired a nuclear missile at the United States, with everything that implies."

There must be a nuclear deterrent put in place regarding this threat equal to the one that worked for so long with the Russians. The only thing keeping certain people from killing all of us immediately is that they can't. In a republic such as ours, where leaders write policies based on the will of the people, it's everybody's job to keep it that way.

"They said Saddam Hussein was crazy when the Gulf War began, but actually, he loves his job, and he wants to keep it, along with his ass and arteries, so when it was made clear to him 'you go biological, we go nuclear,' he got sane real fast."

Volunteers

2001 will always be remembered as the year that the United States, for the first time in decades, found itself in a life-or-death struggle, hoping its citizens would say "How do I help? What can I personally do to stand up to these bastards?"

Well, if you're like most Americans, it's by being extra rude to the Indian family who owns the 7-Eleven. Okay, so our beef isn't exactly with the folks from Bangalore, or Sikhs who practice a different religion entirely, but they're brown-skinned and Middle-Eastern-sounding and…close enough!

"Hey, Mohammed, how much for the Slim Jim?"

Sacrifice used to be commonplace in America—but we're a little out of practice. It's going on three generations since anyone in America was really asked to do squat, even though fake patriots love to say things like "we built this country" to separate themselves from later arriving ethnic groups—as if they built anything. No, the railroads were pretty much up and running by 1980.

President Kennedy's "Ask not…" line is a classic because there was no cynicism in it; it wasn't just political elevator music from the latest corporate empty suit to "lead" us. It was taken literally, by a generation who'd saved the world, listening to a guy who'd been there. The young men who waited on line to enlist for World War II were the children of the Great Depression. They knew about doing their share, accepting hard realities, and going to bed hungry. They got an orange for Christmas and they were damn glad to get it! It was a generation that knew dying isn't the worst thing that can happen to you. Boys as young as 16 and 17 with falsified birth records showed up just out of knickers for the honor of serving their country. If a kid today has a fake ID, it's to get into the Viper Room.

But that's what the Greatest Generation wanted for their kids—to spare them. To give them an easier life than the one they'd been handed. In the process, of course, they ruined them, but hey, it's like the old Chinese proverb says: "One generation plants the tree—another gets the shade." And boy is there a lot of shade out there for the kids today!

What's really scary about them is that they're second and third-generation lazy. "When I was your age, we didn't sit around and watch football. We *played* football…on Nintendo."

But whose fault is it? How can we expect kids who've been brought up on the notion that they're more precious than anything else to suddenly understand living for a nobler ideal? Forget acting like the World War II generation, most of these kids today are such brats, they resent having to even *hear* about the World War II generation. Or anything before MTV. Do you know what anyone under 25 says when you question why they don't know about some monumentally important event in world history? They say, "How should I know about that, I wasn't even born!"

> **Fake patriots love to say things like 'we built this country' to separate themselves from later arriving ethnic groups—as if they built anything. No, the railroads were pretty much up and running by 1980.**

I wasn't born. That's the key, the "I" part. If *I* wasn't around for it, it didn't happen, and it doesn't matter. There's rarely a young adult, even the bright ones, who I talk to and at some point don't think, "I can't believe they let you out of school not knowing that!" And how shameful that my generation, spoiled though we may have been by our supermoms, let our kids grow up decadent and stupid, and all because boomers were spared pain and so *can't take pain*, including the pain of having your kid momentarily hate you because you're *doing the right thing*. Because you're teaching, you're disciplining, you're keeping it real, instead of being your kids' "friend" and negotiating with them and bribing them with empty blandishments and rewards. We give kids trophies for losing and compliments for just existing and tell them "I love you" every five seconds, which is so insecure and annoying.

It's no wonder that to get a young man to even consider enlisting he has to be bribed into it the same way his parents bribed him to clean up his room. The military is forced to lure people in with embarrassing TV commercials that promise adventure and college tuition, or that they can be part of a unit but still remain "an army of one." And if they're really high, there's the one with the ridiculous ruse that being a Marine is pretty much like being in a video game as a knight on a horse fighting exploding dragons.

We've created a culture that makes caring about anything other than yourself seem like losing. The ads talk about joining the army for yourself, your family, your coach, because Grandma got you up for school and made you breakfast (and sometimes took care of your sister's crack baby). What happened to "Do it for your country"? Instead it's like a Bally's gym ad: "You'll get in the best shape of your life."

Immediately following 9/11 it was reported that inquiries to military recruitment offices had skyrocketed. Yeah, the inquiries skyrocketed. The enlistments did not. "Before 9A.M., you say? Listen, I'm getting beeped on the other line."

I was once asked to cut a public service ad against teen smoking, but it never aired because they didn't like what I said, which was:

"Kids, if you think smoking is cool, let me tell you something: you're right. Smoking is cool. It's very cool. Which is why if you need it to be cool, you're not that cool."

I'd like to expand that message to young people today who consider the entitlement of an all-volunteer army to be a birthright and would never think about enlisting because they're too cool for it.

You're not. Oh, we give the military great lip service today—this isn't the 60s when we bashed them to their face. But the proof is in what people do, and increasingly, joining up is simply for those with few other options, so don't tell me the kids think it's cool.

But it is. And there are some people who get that. In fact, I'll tell you about one of them in just a moment.

SPORTS HEROES

Ted Williams

Pat Tillman

Boston Red Sox
1937-1942, 1946-1951, 1954-1960

Arizona Cardinals
1998-2001

REAL HEROES

United States Marines
1943-1945, 1952-1953

US Army, 2002

A Hill of Beans

So much talk, so little action. But, that's the way it has to be if we want to persist in stretching the meaning of "hero" the way we stretch the meaning of everything else in America. If a "suite" is any room in a hotel, and having sex with a girl when she's drunk counts as "rape," then "heroes" can be anyone caught in harm's way.

Except they're not. Victims find themselves in harm's way, heroes put themselves in harm's way. Trapped miners are not heroes; they're guys in a hard job who ran into some bad luck. It's also not heroic to "beat" cancer or prevail in any other endeavor where your motivation is totally saving or advancing your own ass. A hero sacrifices something on purpose, something big. When a culture purposefully blurs that distinction, they're already making excuses for losing.

The airmen who landed our crippled spy plane in China in April of 2000 were lauded as heroes; they may be, but not for that. It's certainly heroic just to choose military service in this prosperous, indulgent society, and for that alone all our servicemen are due our ultimate respect. But the heroic thing to do in the situation over Communist China would have been to *not* land the spy plane with the treasure trove of intelligence data.

"The problems of three little people don't amount to a hill of beans in this world," Humphrey Bogart said in *Casablanca*.

I had to laugh in 1997 when critics kept comparing *Casablanca* to that year's Oscar winner *The English Patient*, because both films involved a man caught between a woman he loved and the greater cause of winning World War II. Of course, in 1943

Circa 1942-1943, Winchester. Created by War Production Board.

the hero—Bogart—chooses *the war* instead of the girl, and in 1996 the "hero" does the exact opposite—a slight change in values.

In the forties, when Ted Williams first gave up his lucrative and magnificent baseball career to go fight the Germans, that was heroism, but it was also routine. Jimmy Stewart was a huge movie star, and he went, as did Gable and Henry Fonda and Tyrone Power and plenty of others. Rich kids, too, like Jack Kennedy and George Herbert Walker Bush, also signed up, because some things were more important than money. Nowadays, we talk a good game about how much we love and support our military personnel, but the truth is it's a mercenary army made up of the poorest members of society with the most limited career choices, who stand up and fight so we don't have to. The public is really no more in touch with the soldiers who protect them than millionaire athletes today are in touch with the fans.

Which is why a Pat Tillman is so impressive. Because Pat Tillman is doing the same thing Ted Williams did, but he's doing it *today*. Today, when a guy would have to be missing the padding in his helmet to even consider giving up the multi-million dollar contracts and the endorsement deals all so he can go eat sand in Crapistan for eighteen grand a year.

But that's exactly what Tillman is doing, having said goodbye to his $1.2-million-dollar-a-year job as the Arizona Cardinals leading tackler.

When it comes to understanding that "hero" is higher than "celebrity," and not the other way around, Pat Tillman gets it. Lots of Americans don't, including the media, who attempt to "celebrify" every legitimate hero of 9/11, and even did it to the first soldier killed in Afghanistan, CIA agent Johnny Spann. You couldn't watch a news broadcast the week he died without seeing some tear-jerk piece about his career and his wife and his three children and exactly where he lived— you know, all the information a dead CIA operative would want out there. Forget that he was a member of a clandestine service or that publicizing his personal life might put his family at risk, the important thing was that we got an *Access Hollywood* segment out of it.

If you don't love Pat Tillman already for leaving football for life, and maybe death, how about this: he did the whole thing, made such a drastic change in his life, without sitting for one interview, or in any way involving the media.

I don't know about you, but that's a hero to me.

"Trapped miners are not heroes; they're guys in a hard job who ran into some bad luck. It's also not heroic to 'beat' cancer or prevail in any other endeavor where your motivation is totally saving or advancing your own ass."

KNOWLEDGE WINS

If You Know the Enemy and Know Yourself

In a widely viewed, and widely praised, television appearance, Dan Rather came on David Letterman's show the first night back after 9/11, and when asked by Dave why—why did it happen—the dean of TV journalism said:

"Who can explain madmen? Who can explain evil?...It's very difficult for anyone in western civilization, much less our United States of America, to understand this type of hate...there's no trying to explain it...some evil just can't be explained."

I guess we were all a little emotional that night—and Dan did keep me in stitches on Election Night, 2000—but still, this is exactly the wrong message.

The Art of War says, "If you know the enemy and know yourself, you need not fear the result of a hundred battles. If you know yourself but not the enemy, for every victory gained you will also suffer a defeat. If you know neither the enemy nor yourself, you will succumb in every battle."

Or, as George C. Scott put it as Patton, "Rommel, you magnificent bastard—I read your book!" What a concept, huh? Learning something. Instead of, "Who knows what the Nazis are like? Let's just attack!"

That approach we tried in Vietnam.

If we agree that 9/11 was a crime on a grand scale, then what kind of criminal are the terrorists? If we say "It's just hate, we can't understand it," then we're saying they're like some insane serial killer. They're John Wayne Gacy, the man who dressed as a clown and buried little boys in his back yard. Who could understand that?

But that's not the kind of criminal the terrorists are. They're a gang, a strong one, with organization, money, motivation and the active support of millions of Muslims around the world, and the tacit support of probably hundreds of millions. "Just hate" won't cut it.

It's not enough anymore to keep referring to a "shadowy enemy." They're shadowy because we don't know anything about them and don't seem particularly interested in finding out. We're not shadowy to them—in fact, we're transparent. They did their homework on us, taking advantage of our weaknesses and our tendencies. They cased the joint, and fit in well enough in a culture they despised (well, it was a love-hate thing, really) to pull off 9/11. Could we do the same in their culture?

Sometimes I want to say to the Muslim world, "Yes, I understand how insulting it is that Americans don't know anything about you, as if you don't matter in the least—but don't take it personally. We don't know anything about *anyone*." Even in our own country—let alone theirs—it's the *local* news we're interested in. There's a half-hour for the network news with that boring, yucky stuff about overseas, and two to three hours of what's going on in the tri-county area, and how to carve a pumpkin.

> **The first President Bush pretended he was dumber than he was by eating pork rinds, all the better to lose the horrible stigma of being a thoughtful Ivy League Eastern establishment type. His son didn't have to pretend quite so much, and was instantly adored for being one of us.**

Does anyone really believe that we can afford, in twenty years' time, to be as dumb as we are now about the part of the world from which this supposedly unfathomable hate is coming? Will airport security in 2025 *still* not be able to tell an Arab from a Mexican? Of course not, because, like they say, war teaches us geography. Also history, religion, economics—all the courses recent college graduates have been allowed to skip so they could study Madonna and Muhammad Ali and vampires and lesbian novels after World War II and porn and how to brew beer. (Those are all real college courses, I couldn't have improved on them comedically if I tried.)

But the learning process will go slowly here because there is no drumbeat for it, in government or the media, because both depend on kissing their voters'/audiences' asses. Americans can only be told they're stupid by surly British people on prime-time torture game shows. Consequently, we revel in our ignorance. We're proud of it. It's a right we've earned by building this country from the ground up. And, once again, by "building this country from the ground up" I mean being born here. The first President Bush pretended he was dumber than he was by eating pork rinds, all the better to lose the horrible stigma of being a thoughtful Ivy League Eastern establishment type. His son didn't have to pretend quite so much, and was instantly adored for being one of us.

Yeah, the presidency, it's only the most important job in the world, why reach for the stars on that one? Let's get a regular Joe. Before 9/11, it was funny that George Bush didn't know where foreign countries were and who ran them, but it's not so funny now. His pre-9/11 policy on the Middle East—basically, Go ahead, kill each other, I'll be on the ranch—seems a little out of step with the times now. Bill Clinton may have been an evil man who likes the ladies, but he sure got it that ignorant disengagement was not an option in the 21st century.

It's easy to just go along to get along, whistling in the dark, lazily placing blind faith in our leadership. The war is a scary thing, and for some folks, George Bush became a genius on September 12, and there's no need to take a re-look-see at that! People say, "I'm not interested in politics," like it's just another hobby, like "I'm not into skiing or needlepoint."

But freedom isn't free. It shouldn't be a bragging point that, "Oh, I don't get involved in politics," as if that makes you somehow cleaner. No, that makes you derelict of duty in a republic. Liars and panderers in government would have a much harder time of it if so many people didn't insist on their right to remain ignorant and blindly agreeable.

And foreign adversaries would have to calculate the savvy of our people into their nefarious plans.

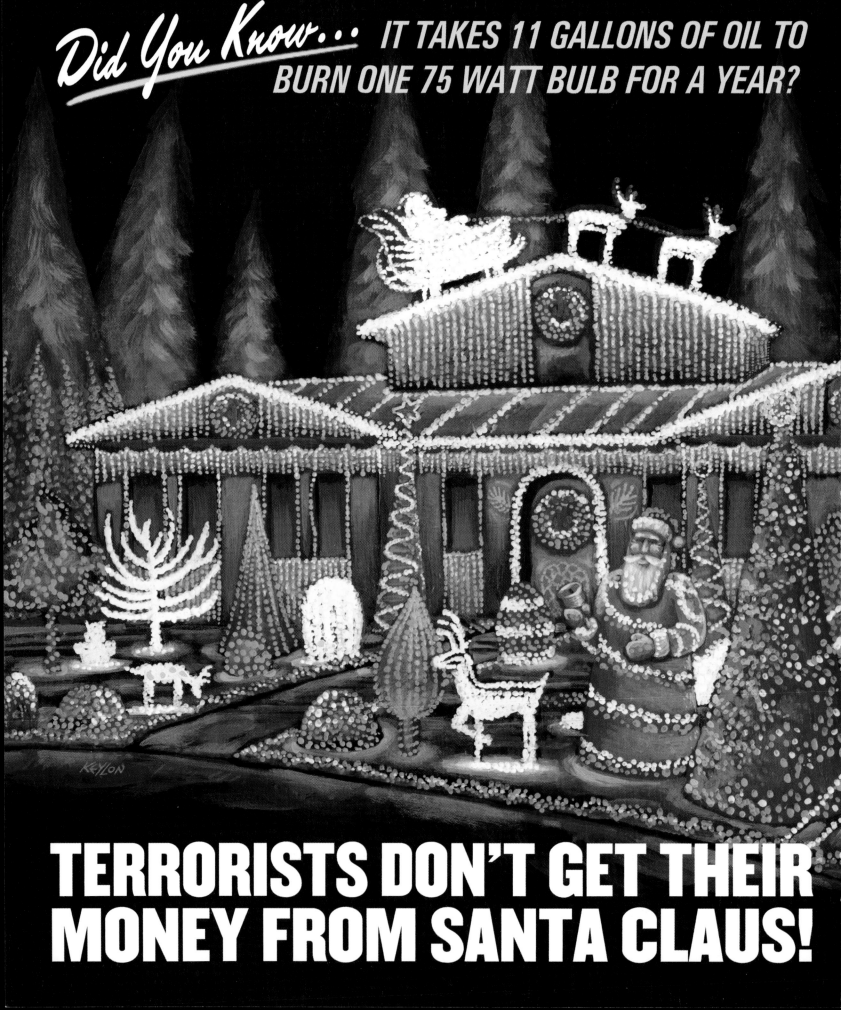

The Lamp You Don't Turn Off

Question: Where do terrorists get the money to live in their fancy caves? That's right, from rich, oil-producing countries. And where do the oil-producing countries get the money? From us buying oil. Yes, it really does take eleven gallons of oil to light one 75-watt bulb for a year. We don't think of oil as being involved when we light a lamp or leave the television on all day, but it is.

I don't know if every time a bell rings an angel gets his wings, but it's a fact that every time a Christmas display goes up, more money pours into Saudi Arabia—you know, our "ally" (wink, wink). And the Saudis and the United States have something in common. Well, two things if you count the sick co-dependency with oil and cash. The other thing we have in common is Osama bin Laden's hatred for both of us—them for letting us in the Holy Land, and us for being *in* the Holy Land. It's something about the Holy Land.

Give this to bin Laden: he keeps it real about what's actually bugging him and his kind: filthy, dirty infidels—Jews and Americans—in the Holy Land, there, of course, to protect the oil. This is a crowd that will tell you right to your face that they hate your friggin' guts and think you're irredeemable, so you really must go. Which is what we, and by "we" I mean I, really think about them and their financial patrons, i.e., the Saudis, who bribe bin Laden to hate us slightly more than them.

And that bribe money comes from us, because to us, the Holy Land isn't the holy land—it's the oily land, and after seeing Saddam Hussein almost take it over in 1991, we're not about to let it go unguarded again. Now, we wouldn't need to guard it at all if we weren't constantly fiending for oil, but we're talkin' to a junkie here. And a junkie's first answer to a problem isn't "give up the dope"—it's "how can I make this work and keep doing dope." That's what we want to do—win a war against people backed by oil money, but do it without bringing oil into the equation. Because, as I've said, we love our cars more than we love each other and we'd hump them if we could.

Which brings me to Christmas lights. I can't tell you how many people I talked to last December who thought they were actually *helping* the war effort by having monstrous front lawn displays. Why did they think it was a help? Well, they were a little fuzzier on that. Something about "or else they win" and a big slice of "it makes me *feel* better," which, after all, is the goal of any war machine. To make us feel better. Us. Not the kid from the ghetto or poor rural town who's in the army guarding the oil.

I hate to say it, but we used to win to feel better, and now we feel better to win.

Which isn't to say around the holidays things can't be festive, they can—I'm not a Communist. But folks, there's a war on. Not to mention that Christmas is supposed to be a reverent, spiritual and, yes, joyous celebration of the everlasting life and love of the Son of God—it's not a competition. If Christmas is really about Jesus, why does your front lawn have to be Jesus in Las Vegas? Should a crèche really be electric? Does everything on the lawn have to light up and move? Santas and sleighs and reindeer and snowmen and elves and 12-foot candy canes and toy soldiers and Little Drummer Boys and trains, all with movable parts and sound-effects of birds chirping and bells ringing and Santa, in stereo, with his back-up singers the Ho, Ho, Hos. Christ, if bin Laden doesn't like what's going on in the real Holy Land, he should check out the one at the corner of Sunset and Alpine.

It's not only gaudy and tacky, it just encourages people to go out driving around looking at Christmas lights, wasting even more oil!

My father, who grew up in the Depression and seemed to think the American economy hadn't changed much into the sixties, used to fine my sister and me a nickel every time we left a room with the light on. It doesn't seem like much, but then again our allowance was fifty cents a week. If only the people who ran stores had kept prices at their 1935 level, he would have been a happy guy. And I could have afforded a few more baseball cards. But to this day, I do not leave lights on when I leave a room, not even in a hotel.

Remember, we here in the States aren't going to make a difference by getting a flashlight and a plane ticket and going over there and searching for the bad people cave by cave. It's all the little things we can do here that add up—it's the lamp you don't turn off that down the road gets a guy killed. I guess what I'm saying is, use the battery-powered "personal massaging devices" instead of the ones that plug into the wall. And this holiday season, make sure the only thing lit on your lawn is a disoriented Robert Downey, Jr.

Merry Christmas!

"We used to win to feel better, and now we feel better to win."

WHICH SUICIDE ARE YOU WORRIED ABOUT?
TELL THEM IN WASHINGTON!
PROTECT US FROM EVIL, NOT FROM OURSELVES

Eye On the Ball

Before 9/11, our government got involved in protecting us from all sorts of hazards, from the Budweiser frog to asbestos, from road rage to Internet porn and Bill Clinton's penis. And by watching the nightly news, you'd think the greatest threat to our personal safety was either shark attacks or mold. But then came our 9/11 "wake-up call," and everything...

Please. If everything changed, how come we're still fighting the old, stupid wars alongside the real war? Why are decent citizens still being jailed for smoking the wrong plant, easing the suffering of the terminally ill, or accepting cash for sex instead of the customary dinner and drinks?

Politicians love to talk about the wisdom of the people in their ass-kissing stump speeches, but apparently these wise people are not even smart enough to decide when they can die. Which is ironic, because the two things that bring the most wisdom in life are pain and age—and most people who want to end it usually have plenty of both. How annoying it must be for such people, old and in pain, to have young, arrogant "lawmakers" making life and death decisions for them.

The adult, right-minded patients requesting physician-assisted suicides are not victims of their doctors, they're victims of their illnesses. The doctors are humanely facilitating the inevitable, helping those dying in agony to make their exit with dignity, either by providing prescription medication, or the old-fashioned way, by showing them the bill. We wouldn't think of allowing our pets or racehorses to needlessly suffer before an inescapable death. Why not be just as "humane" to people? Isn't the choice to accept death with dignity a precious personal freedom and a far cry better than sitting in a Craftmatic adjustable bed with a tube in your nose trying to eat a puzzle?

Which brings me to the Nimitzes. In early 2002, Chester W. Nimitz, Jr., son of the famed World War II admiral and a highly decorated admiral in his own right, killed himself in a double suicide with his wife, Joan, in what I like to call the Irrefutable Argument for Assisted Suicide.

The Nimitzes had everything: a good life, honors and real honor, a loving marriage, good kids—everything that defines a happy life for most people. And then they didn't, because they got old. Robust into their 80s, at some point the body goes—it just does. It's not designed for forever. Life became a chore of just staying alive, and that's no life at all. Maybe if the Nimitzes had led dull, inactive lives, like the weenies who write stupid laws, then the transition to droolitude wouldn't have been so hard to take. But they *lived*, so just hanging on wasn't an option. They had lost their mobility, then their health, and finally, most sadly, the remote.

They told the kids their plans, said the key good-byes, put all their affairs in absolutely apple-pie order, and then shuffled off their mortal coil together, quietly and with dignity. Having led a good life, they weren't afraid to die. Spiritual people never are. It's the religious who are more often afraid to bring on the afterparty. Then they project that fear on others, like the Nimitzes, who would have been stopped if they had gotten so infirm they couldn't do it themselves.

Mr. President, and everyone else there in Washington, get your noses out of our personal affairs. Stop trying to police the private, adult decisions we make in our bedrooms, our doctors' offices or section 29, row L of a Nelly concert. Read the *Enquirer*, do something else to scratch that itch. Get a life. You have a big, big job now, and frankly, you're not so good you can do it distracted.

"Why are decent citizens still being jailed for smoking the wrong plant, easing the suffering of the terminally ill, or accepting cash for sex instead of the customary dinner and drinks?"

NATIONAL PUBLIC RADIO QUESTIONNAIRE
JULY 23-25, 2002

WHICH OF THE FOLLOWING ISSUE AREAS WOULD BE MOST IMPORTANT IN DECIDING HOW TO VOTE FOR A CANDIDATE FOR CONGRESS? (TOP TWO CHOICES)

35% THE ECONOMY AND JOBS

24% SOCIAL SECURITY AND MEDICARE

23% EDUCATION

21% AFFORDABLE HEALTH CARE

16% MORAL VALUES

16% Anti-terrorism Efforts

12% TAXES

12% FEDERAL SPENDING

9% CORPORATE ABUSE

8% THE ENVIRONMENT

7% CRIME AND ILLEGAL DRUGS

Wrong Answer!

Something and Nothing

Because the subject of history in high school and college has become a kind of fun create-your-own potpourri of whatever silly peripheral knowledge you want to pretend you're studying, we're now several generations removed from the important idea that we should at least try to learn from our past. It was less than a century ago that government was expected to do far less for its citizens than it does today. No federal income tax was assessed before 1913, because government didn't require the kind of dough it needs now that it's running a concierge business. What it was expected to do was protect the people, with an army for foreigners, and police for crooks. No endowing of artists, no welfare for fat cats, no making sure the drawstring on your kid's pajamas doesn't strangle him.

One politician got it exactly right the week of September 11. Curt Weldon, Republican congressman from Pennsylvania, said: "It's a tragedy that it took the loss of thousands of lives to wake this country up and realize that our number one responsibility is not education—and I'm a teacher—and it's not health care, and I'm married to a nurse. It is in fact the security and safety of the American people."

Remember that when you're in the voting booth. Stop voting for the officials who offer us the biggest tax cut and the longest paternity leave, and start electing the ones committed to security first at any cost. Remember that the primary function of government is protection: to handle the kind of threats only they can handle. I can't build a nuclear missile or an Apache helicopter, so I don't mind when my tax dollars go to buy them, because I know they're necessary to deter or repel the savages who exist outside, and sometimes inside, our moat. Of course it would be nice to excise the corrupt waste and pilfering that goes on in military culture, but until we do, there's no choice but to live with it, so that we have a Pentagon and an army that scares the crap out of people.

Only one year after an attack as vicious and foreboding as September 11, for so many voters to be so badly prioritizing is very frightening. It's as if on September 11 our heads all came up, like grazing deer who heard a snapping twig. Senses heightened, adrenaline pumping, we stood silently for a moment on full alert, knowing that there was danger near.

And then we went back to grazing. Grazing in our private and convenient little world of consumption and entitlement, encouraged to do so by a government that actually told its citizens in wartime to shop, go out to eat, and, for God's sake, travel! "Go ahead, get away," they insisted, "We'll handle the war; you've been through enough."

> **People keep saying, 'we need to remember September 11.' Yeah, but what we really need to remember is how we felt right after September 11, those heady few weeks when we couldn't believe how petty we'd been in the past, or how perfectly Seinfeld had captured the zeitgeist of the 90s—because it turned out everything back then really _was_ about nothing!**

After the attacks, our president said this about the terrorists: "They underestimated us."

No, sir, _you_ did.

Our government's first mistake was treating us like victims instead of soldiers in the war on terror. Typical of a system where the political tail wags the dog of state, the answer to war is: if the happy ending is hearing the "all-clear" signal, then why not just start with that?

Somewhere along the line, the people became the leaders and the leaders became the led. "Poll driven" is a great phrase because it brings to mind a great plain, across which is being _driven_ a dumb herd—you know, Congress and the President, who decide policy not by what's best for America and its future, but by crunching the numbers and establishing the path of least resistance to re-election. One might think that an approval rating above eighty—which President Bush enjoyed for a full six months after the attacks—would be cushion enough to spend a little political capital on "givin' it to us straight;" after all, for a short time we were actually ready to accept it.

But politicians don't do that anymore. Ronald Reagan could have brought America to a sensible place about guns after he got shot—not even the NRA could have fought a popular new president with a bullet in his chest if he said, "Hey, we all love guns, but let's admit the framers had in mind militias with muskets, not urban gangs with machine pistols. And besides, I just got shot." But the moment passed. And now the moments after 9/11 seem like a long, long time ago.

Because our leaders now follow us, it is therefore up to us to set our national priorities. As long as we signal that the economy, education, or banning cell phones in cars is more important to us than national security, then that's exactly where our pandering, finger-in-the-wind government will focus our resources.

People keep saying, "we need to remember September 11." Yeah, but what we really need to remember is how we felt right *after* September 11, those heady few weeks when we couldn't believe how petty we'd been in the past, or how perfectly Seinfeld had captured the zeitgeist of the 90s—because it turned out everything back then really *was* about nothing! Impeachment was nothing! Elian Gonzalez was nothing! Gays in the military, smoking in movies, childproofing Las Vegas—it was all nothing! We all came to our senses for five minutes and realized how nothing it all was and how much a new set of priorities was in order.

And then we forgot again.

Don't waste food while others starve!

To Die For

Five months after the attacks, the Fox network broadcast the first installment of *The Glutton Bowl*. It was exactly what it sounded like: an eating contest from the world's biggest pigs. Who wants to marry a Frigidaire? And it was widely laughed off or admired because OR ELSE THEY WIN!

We just don't get it. We cannot, for the life of us, figure out why a world where half the people go to bed hungry every night would find such a thing rude—the equivalent of standing in front of a homeless guy with a sandwich and tossing it onto a passing garbage truck, instead of leaving it for him in the dumpster.

We not only waste an extraordinary amount of food, we also play with it and pre-vent it from being grown. We wrestle in Jell-O while poorer nations' exotic dancers are forced to square off in mud. Our mindset is "If you've got it, flaunt it"—not "if you've got it, share it." And we pretend being religious makes us moral and charitable.

But the charitable don't gorge for fun while others forage for scraps. Whatever happened to "there are people starving in China"?

Hamburger ads say "If it doesn't get all over the place, it doesn't belong in your face"—and that's a selling point. We shop with fork-lifts. We eat giant food off of giant plates. We have a national holiday where we *stuff food into other food*. We demand food immediate-ly, and in the car, so we can eat, shop, and pollute the atmosphere all at the same time. We eat on planes, trains and automo-biles and everywhere in between. We even take our wife out to a nice Italian meal before shooting her in the head—allegedly.

FOOD IS A WEAPON

DON'T WASTE IT !
BUY WISELY - COOK CAREFULLY - EAT IT ALL

FOLLOW THE NATIONAL WARTIME NUTRITION PROGRAM

Circa 1941-1945. Created by Office of Government Reports. United States Information Service. Division of Public Inquiry. Bureau of Special Services, OWI.

Even our poor people are fat.

Food is so abundant here people staple their stomach shut so they won't kill themselves from gorging on it—and then, of course, this being America, are afforded the kind of reception normally reserved for somebody who'd been shot down behind enemy lines, for their "courage" and "discipline." Roseanne tried the procedure without success, but that's because cows have five stomachs.

By the way, whatever happened to the old-fashioned way of losing weight: liposuction and months of nonstop freebasing?

> **// Hamburger ads say 'If it doesn't get all over the place, it doesn't belong in your face'—and that's a selling point. We shop with forklifts. We eat giant food off of giant plates. We have a national holiday where we *stuff food into other food.* //**

America represents less than 5% of the world's population, yet we consume 30% of its resources. We are bogarting the earth. We could feed the world with just the garnish off our plates, and yet we pay farmers not to grow crops. We actually produce more than enough grain to feed every person on earth, but the part of it we don't let rot to keep prices up we feed to our livestock so we can enjoy meaty, inefficient diets that sap our resources, deteriorate our organs and pollute more groundwater than industry.

And make no mistake, it *is* about the poverty. Many times I've heard the argument, "the 9/11 hijackers were not poor," and many of them weren't. But that doesn't mean poverty isn't a root cause of terrorism. Hungry people tend to follow the ideology of those willing to feed them and resent those who don't. Desperate, poor young Muslim men in many countries are sponsored by wealthy Saudi Arabia, which is guided by the fanatical Wahhabi sect, to attend madrasses, which are hotbeds of Muslim fanaticism and anti-American indoctrination. They go for the room and board, they stay for the hate.

Of course, we'll probably beat them to killing us, because that's what gluttony does to people. It kills them. There's a reason why the top-selling prescription drugs in America are all different chemical elixirs for ulcers, bloating, indigestion, high cholesterol—because no one ever says to Americans, "Maybe you should change your diet." There's money in eating badly, and there's money in the pills that put out the fires set by eating badly.

Cardiovascular disease is our number-one killer; cancer is number two; diabetes is up 40% in the past decade, and American adults have a 61% obesity rate. Even kids here are fat little eating machines—half of them look like Pugsly. And why not, schools teach acceptance above all: "Love Your Body Day." How about a "Delaying Gratification for Future Well-being Day"?

It is a terrible irony, not lost I'm sure on many of our most fervid haters, that we are dying of over-consumption, and they of under-consumption. As a great comedian once said, if only Mama Cass had shared her sandwich with Karen Carpenter, there'd be two more singers alive today.

TANNED, RESTED and READY

The War Continues

Nothing But Time

There's an old Russian proverb that says, "Not everyone who snores is sleeping"—and boy do horny, married guys know that. It also applies to our current enemy. Even though there was a lull in the attack on America after September 11, there's still a war going on. We need to remember that. We're not safe, and it's not over. And it's not going to be over in our lifetime, unless we're at the end of a thousand-year struggle.

The people of the Muslim world, like most people outside the United States, have much longer memories than we do. We're a young country with a short history, and even that has proved too much of a challenge to keep alive now that we stopped teaching our children actual knowledge and facts. Not so in the coffee-houses of Damascus or Cairo. To folks in this part of the world, the thirteenth century was last Friday. Milosevic in Yugoslavia stirred the pot against the Kosovars back in 1989 because it was the anniversary of a battle the Serbs lost to the encroaching—weren't they always?—Muslims.

The *600th* anniversary. And it resonated.

During the Gulf War, Saddam Hussein had some of his billboards—he's the Angelyne of Baghdad—changed to make him look like Salahadin, the Muslim hero who retook Jerusalem in *1187*. But ask anyone in America under 100 to write an essay on why George Washington really earned his nickname. (The Father of our Country, for those under fifty.)

Not only do dictators have more time to work with than we do, they also have more bodies. Saddam famously said he would win the contest with America in 1991 because we couldn't stomach the thought of 50,000 dead in one battle, and he was right. He, however, being the virile, manly strongman he is, can stomach the thought of thousands of dead. It's almost a prerequisite for dictators. Stalin was such a strong leader, he was able to stomach *twenty million* of his own people dying in World War II. As Melanie Griffith once said when they had to explain the Holocaust to her for a movie role: "That's a lot of people!"

Since the Second Intifada, the Israelis have lost the population equivalent of our 9/11 body count every ten weeks.

Which is all just to say that the world is a bad place with bad men, and some of the worst of them are not through with us. The terrorists weren't just a radical fringe group who have since been rounded up and disposed of, and we certainly haven't caved to their demands, pulling all our troops from the Holy Land and telling Israel to go piss up a rope. It's not like 9/11 was one of those socially embarrassing, impulsive outbursts and now they've got it all out of their system and they're in anger-management class. They're sure of their cause and their objectives, and they're about as self-righteous as you can get without actually sitting on the board of the *700 Club*. And every day Charlie spends in the jungle, he gets stronger.

> **We're engaged with an enemy that strikes intermittently, every few years—kind of like baseball players.**

We're engaged with an enemy that strikes intermittently, every few years—kind of like baseball players. They rely on the element of surprise and depend upon our complacency. It's not enough for us to count on strictly defensive measures—tightening our borders and increasing airport security. The defensive approach in military tactics always loses. All lines are ultimately Maginot lines. The best defense is offense, scaring people into not trying anything. Covering up, as under a magical space shield, and saying, "You can't get at me" never wins. They always can.

"If history teaches us anything," Michael Corleone said, "it's that you can kill anyone."

And the folks that have been killing Americans lately don't see our annihilation as a rush job. If you've seen the footage of Osama bin Laden, he always has a serene, confident look on his face, like he just communed with Allah or got blown. It's a look that seems to say, "Death to America, but all in good time."

Americans have trouble relating to the idea of "in good time." As Carrie Fisher once wrote, instant gratification would be fine except it takes too long. The idea of having to wait centuries to achieve a goal is just preposterous to us.

But this war that we call The War on Terrorism, this new war against a new foe, really isn't new. It certainly isn't new to the people we're fighting. The war they're fighting has been going on since Pope Urban II declared the first Crusade in 1095. The struggle going on now for Jerusalem is seen as a battle first waged against western Crusaders. Ariel Sharon is just the latest Godfrey of Bologne or Richard the Lionhearted, sent off by infidels like Pope Urban or George Bush to secure their client-state outpost in the Middle East. What the infidels call themselves— crusaders, Israelis, Americans—is unimportant. The intervals of time are unimportant. What's important is winning.

We get through a year of no attacks and sound the all-clear. They reload and wait. As the months roll on beyond 9/11, let's all try to remember: it's not over when we say it's over. It's over when they say it's over.

Watching What We Say

In early 2002, pressure was building in the Democratic Party for someone to say something about...well, anything really. Since the attacks in September, the government in power had done a good job of casting any dissenting opinion as ill-timed and unpatriotic. Have a question or a comment? Get in the line over there marked "Al Qaeda Operatives."

But finally Senate majority leader Tom Daschle, firebrand that he is, rose in the Senate well and said:

"Before we make commitments in resources, I think we need to have a clearer understanding of what the direction will be."

Wow. You go, girl. What a gauntlet to throw down—the leader of the party that got the most votes in the last election asking, "So what's next?"

But the other party was outraged. Tom DeLay called Daschle's remarks "disgusting." Really? The leader of the Congress, the body of government assigned by the constitution to appropriate funds, asking what they'll be used for—that's "disgusting?"

I've never understood people who interpret the Bible literally, and the constitution loosely.

Trent Lott was also indignant, so much so that his hair almost moved. He said, "How dare Senator Daschle criticize President Bush while we are fighting our war on terrorism, especially when we have troops in the field?" Tom Davis, R-VA., said Daschle's comments "have the effect of giving aid and comfort to our enemies." I assumed he meant the Democrats.

Hey, you're either with us or against us.

But come on, America can't have it that only one party is allowed to play politics and speak out—it'll completely unbalance our corrupt system of crony capitalism. Plus, "with us or against us," when misapplied to our own loyal opposition, is more like what we're fighting, and less like what we're fighting for. One of the great strengths of this country is our ability to examine matters of national policy in the court of public opinion. But we panic and forget that, time after time. I myself had the honor of being scolded by the president's spokesman with the words "Americans need to watch what they say...."

Yeah, if you're giving away state secrets. But otherwise, not having to watch what you say is why we love it here, or it should be. Having to "watch it" is what stinks about living under the Taliban or the KGB or the Stasis. Our problem with free speech in America is, we've taken away so much of it voluntarily through the enforced appropriateness of political correctness, that when a high official says "watch what you say," we think:

"So what?! Hell, watching what you say is what life in America is like anyway, at least if you work in an office and want to stay married."

By the way, for someone who almost always has a dissenting opinion, my comment about the 9/11 kamikaze pilots not being cowards was, ironically, not dissent at all. The dissenting opinion in the aftermath of 9/11 was "We shouldn't go to war in Afghanistan." Now, I've always been for giving war a chance and more good, hard U.S. military ass-kickings to any Gangsta government on any continent, be it Hussein, Milosevic, Noriega, Adid, or the Taliban. Or Quaddafi, just for old time's sake.

> **Athenians made Socrates drink the hemlock, but not because his warnings about their downfall had been mistaken; he was right, and they hated him for it. Kind of like Al Gore in a toga.**

No, what I said was not dissent but an uncomfortable truth, which is different. That's more about timing, and it's another reason we desperately need to fight for free speech in wartime. Because people who get in trouble for what they say aren't necessarily wrong. Athenians made Socrates drink the hemlock, but not because his warnings about their downfall had been mistaken; he was right, and they hated him for it. Kind of like Al Gore in a toga. The Smothers Brothers got thrown off TV in 1969 for saying the Vietnam War was immoral and un-winnable. By 1979 that was such an accepted mainstream opinion you'd have a hard time finding someone to argue the reverse—although I have, and do.

The problem in America is not too much speaking out—it's too little. We're not overrun with rebels here, we're overrun with sheep. We need more people, not less, to say out loud what at least some others are thinking. We need raw honesty especially in an age where we cannot expect statesmanship. Government can be trusted less than ever to tell the truth, because they are owned more than ever by moneyed interests whose interest is money and not truth. The United States government should be telling you the things I've been saying—not me! *They* should be making the case to conserve fuel, pay the full tax load, boycott diamonds—but they don't, because they can't.

They talk of integrity, but their idea of it is not to betray their donors.

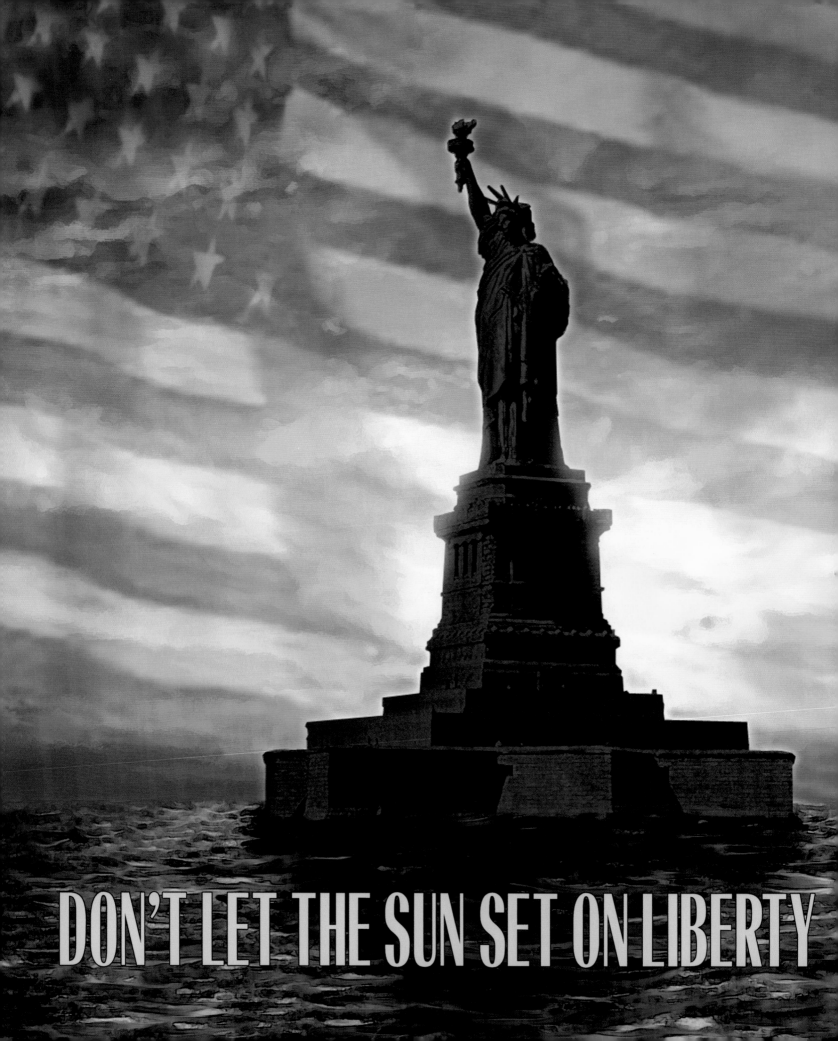

Not Just Different

In the fall of 2001, the lowlife, traitorous ingrate in America was the guy arguing "America is the greatest nation on earth," when everyone knew it was the greatest nation *ever* on earth. The all-time champion civilization, because coming out on top of a pissing match with the 8th century Mayans—that's what's important.

As I'm sure you know by now, I'm not much for tradition or sentiment—but America doesn't need sentiment to make its case as the greatest nation on earth, right now anyway, and that's good enough for me. I'll deal with the Ming Dynasty later, and perhaps stop there for lunch.

I've tried to stress a few concepts in this book: making connections; keeping in mind that government's first job is protection; and perspective. Americans love to say "this is the greatest country on earth!" but they're just pulling that out of their ass; there is no perspective. They have not traveled extensively overseas, nor have they done exhaustive, life-index factor by life-index factor studies of the United States vs. Belgium or Sweden or Luxembourg. The health care system may very well be better in Germany, and the weather in Spain beats Buffalo, and I *know* I like the pot laws better in Holland. The truth is, people are inert by nature, and most think their place of origin is superior because they're used to it.

But there is no denying America is Rome at this moment in history, and that in itself is greatness. Even greater is having the power of Rome and also a record, comparable to other pre-eminent powers, of remarkably mute brutality. No country with comparable power ever trod so gently on the rest of the world, something foreigners often pretend they don't know, but they do. They do because other countries still teach their damn kids history!—which will tell you that in any era, it's some country's turn to be "the man" on this planet: the Egyptians, the Greeks, the Romans, the Mongols, the Arabs, the Spanish, the French, the English—even the Iraqis (Babylonia)—everybody gets a turn to carry the big stick, and when they do, they've all behaved even worse than we have.

A nation with the power of the United States can't be expected to never get its uniform a little dirty—but attention must be paid to perspective. Rome didn't have a big terrorism problem because when someone would piss them off, they'd *kill all the men and sow salt in the earth so nothing would ever grow there again*. That's a conservative. America does not go to war to rob or exterminate or get even; we don't conquer, we don't plunder, and we don't carry off anyone's women and children into slavery and concubining. Name another nation that could conquer the world, but chose not to. A lot of nations have tried, and usually for one reason: they could. They found themselves—like America is now—pre-eminent. And that big stick in their hand was just too much fun not to use.

America does, as I have not flinched from pointing out in this book, practice a kind of passive-aggressive violence on the world's poor, driven by our gluttony and myopia—that's bad, and people die from it. But "American foreign policy" and "the Palestinian situation" are the "dog ate my homework" and "my parents screwed me up" of political excuses. I am so tired of hearing about the brutality of America's foreign policy from a culture that conquered the world in a century. They say Islam means peace, and I know to hundreds of millions it does, but it is also a religion that was born a conqueror. From the death of Mohammad in 632 to the Battle of Tours in 732, the army coming out of the Arabian desert "converted" half the world in a only one hundred years, and you don't do that by handing out flyers and singing "Kumbaya."

> **I am so tired of hearing about the brutality of America's foreign policy from a culture that conquered the world in a century. From the death of Mohammad in 632 to the Battle of Tours in 732, the army coming out of the Arabian desert 'converted' half the world in a only one hundred years, and you don't do that by handing out flyers and singing 'Kumbaya.'**

The relevant comparison between the United States and the Muslim world should be from our time of ascendancy, now, to their time of ascendancy, in the late Middle Ages. How "compassionate" was the foreign policy of the Seljuk Turks or the Abbasid caliphate during the time when they were carrying the big stick? It's easy to claim moral superiority when you are a powerless nation—hey, without that the U.N. would just be a lot of black guys with good parking spots in New York. It's easy to be a powerless country and have lofty, unattainable ideals—that's all you have. Just the stuff people dream of, like, you know, driving every Israeli into the sea.

But powerful nations should be judged differently in the world contest. Powerful nations have *opportunities* to be bad. They have options. It's like with men: only as loyal as their options. Contrary to feminist nonsense, Mick Jagger doesn't have "Peter Pan complex," he just has *options* unavailable to the average Mack who's *sixty*. In the same way, America has the *option* to settle nearly everything with brute power, but it doesn't. Like we couldn't just *take* the oil? Please. I'm not saying that makes us saints for passing on the absolute lowest, most selfish road. I'm saying it makes us, right now, better than them. I'm saying that, among the Seljuk Turks, "Should we take the oil?" is not even a discussion.

America is not a blameless nation: indeed, our challenge at the Pearly Gates will be about what we did to our *own* people (genocide and slavery are not misdemeanors in heaven.) But does anyone really say, Gee, what would the world be like if Saddam Hussein or any of the amoral despots who run so many countries had the big nuclear capability and America was Canada? Should we try it that way?

Frighteningly, millions around the world would say yes. I have foreign friends who, when they hear me speak, scoff and say, "America just does its own brand of conquering." Yes, exactly, and our brand is better. Yes, we plunder with our "cultural imperialism," boo hoo; I'm guessing that's better than the Genghis Khan-Joseph Stalin variety. Our soldiers are stationed in the Holy Land? Your warlord's henchmen are in your sister's bedroom.

And while we're at it, can we stop with "American cultural imperialism?" Harry Potter is English, Pokemon is Japanese, soccer is just awful. Does anyone really expect the United States, which has, through hard work and ingenuity become the lone superpower, to have its effect felt *nowhere* in the world? The steps of the world's giant should be so soft that no one can even hear them? We have the power of Rome, but the big crisis is you're eating our crappy fast food?

World history is really all about timing. It is lucky to be an American in the last half of the 20th century, and we should never forget that. If you are, it means you're one of the blessed people born in the right country at the right time. In the 13th century, you'd want to be a Mongolian; in the 15th century BC, an Egyptian; in the ninth a Frank. Islam in the Middle Ages was far superior to European civilization, having medicine, math and astronomy while whitey was shivering behind castle walls and dying at 30.

But they stopped, and we didn't. We edited, and self-corrected. We had a renaissance and an enlightenment, and they didn't.

Everyone in the world isn't just "different," as politically correct multiculturalism would have you believe. That's the kind of thinking that lets people get away with keeping women in the beekeeper suits! Freedom of religion, representative democracy, religious and ethnic tolerance, equality of the sexes, rule of law, free speech—these things aren't just different from beheadings and stonings and autocracy—they're *better*.

"We have our extremists and fundamentalists, too," I hear people say. Yeah, but America is a great country because our kooks and nuts are funny, not scary! They do things like accuse puppets on television shows of being gay because they're purple, and everyone laughs. Jerry Falwell and Pat Robertson think homos burn in hell, but they don't suggest we drag Richard Simmons into the public square and cut off his head!

I'm suggesting it. In fact, I'm insisting on it.

September 11, it was said, united all Americans, and in some ways it did—but if what allows two American strangers to sing our anthem together is a common belief that this is the greatest country, that's not enough. We have to also agree on *why* it's the greatest country, and it's not because the toilets flush like typhoons.

If there's one thing we've heard a lot since 9/11—besides how easy it is for firemen to get laid—it's that "we're at a crossroads." Politicians love to say "we're at a crossroads" because it makes their meaningless election as the Republicrat representing the whiners of wherever seem crucial, though it's usually not. But September 11? That is a crossroads. It is a real threat, a real gut check, a real test of how we respond. A politician—or any type of panderer—always says "America will prevail." But that is the expression of a wish, not the basis for policy. Because if you believe that our prevailing is assured, then your policy would be to do nothing, and many have.

Obviously, that's not the approach this book has endorsed. I am proud to be Western. To be pro-active. To respect fate, but not be passive about my future. I believe we will prevail, but I don't believe it's pre-ordained. I know God blesses America, and loves us best, but maybe He's going to get another girlfriend in the future. After all, He dumped England for us, and Spain for England, and Holland for Spain and so on and so on. And even if we are different and are in fact the real, true Manifest Destiny Chosen People—let's act like we're not, just in case. Just to cover our asses.

My favorite movie is *Saving Private Ryan*, and at the end of it a dying Tom Hanks tells the saved private, "Earn this." I try to remember that every day, and put myself in Ryan's place. We're all a little intoxicated with just being Americans, but even better would be to *earn it*. And kill the world with kindness, because it will make us safer, and even greater.

We've been the greatest country on earth for two centuries. Let's Three-peat!